This book is dedicated to the heroic Christians who understand that life is ministry and live like it. May you continue to represent Jesus in a way that pleases Him and blesses all His Creation.

CHURCH DISTRIBUTED

How the Church Can Thrive in the Coming Era of Connection

Church Distributed

© 2007 JOEL C. HUNTER
ISBN 978-1-60402-615-3 (Soft Cover $14.99)
    978-1-60402-647-4 (Hard Cover $19.99)

Published by Distributed Church Press,
530 Dog Track Road, Longwood, Florida 32750

Table of Contents

Acknowledgements

To say that this book was a collaborative effort is an understatement. Some of the chief contributors, in addition to the authors I've read, are the people who perfect me: I appreciate my family. Becky, you are the ideal wife for me, and the perfect mother for our sons and their wives. Your unwavering devotion has made our family indivisible, our individual gifts evident, and our life together a joy.

Josh, I wish I had your wisdom and maturity. Isaac, I wish I had your insight and leadership capability. Joel, I wish I had your intelligence and discipline. Lisa, I need a dose of your social skills. Rhonda, I could do with a modicum of your elegance. Lizzy, your wit and resolve inspire me. But since I have only a smattering of all of these qualities, and since I am not myself without you, I will depend on you staying very close to your mom and to me.

I am blessed by wonderful friends: Vernon and Connie Rainwater, Tim and Eleanor Tracey, Randall and Julie Loy, and Reggie Kidd from days of old, I could not ask for better ministry partners or better examples of how differences make us complete. Northland elders and ministry leaders, thanks for developing the church while I'm living in the future.

Special thanks to all who loaned me places of escape to write this book: my dear sister and brother-in-law, Michele and Jan Graves; Brian and Dianne Walsh; Ken and Linda Koldenhoven; and, from the old days, Jean and Bill Maroletti. And to those who worked through this manuscript with me: Becky, Robert Andrescik, Andy Butcher, Matthew Green, Andrew Greenberg, Doug Trouten and Jimmy Stewart.

The "we could not do this without each other" awards go to the staff and congregation of Northland Church along with the leaders of several of our first linked churches; in New Hampshire, Christ Church of Amherst; Egypt, Kasr El Dobara; Namibia, Khomas Community Church; South Africa, Vredelust; Sri Lanka, Kithu Sevana; Ukraine, Dom Architectora. Jim Laird, thanks for your tremendous service as our first Ambassador-at-Large for Partnerships in Global Ministries.

Team support is a form of personal support. In the best places of work, we can't tell them apart. My fellow pastors and elders at Northland are outstanding leaders who have envisioned the future with me, while paying attention to the needs of our congregation. They guide our church as true shepherds, and I depend on them. Heartfelt kudos to Pastor Lon Garber, our first distributed pastor, and his wife, Val, who moved to Namibia to enable the distributed church vision in that African nation.

The staff and congregation of Northland are my extended family. Their competence has allowed me to focus; their ministry has prompted and completed my teaching. The paid and volunteer ministers, and the congregation that acts as the church distributed and supports pioneering efforts in outside relationships are all "letters of recommendation" for this arrangement of church.

I am so grateful for various people who were probably unaware of their impact on my life. They have been friends and teachers: Mrs. Wolfe and Miss Joy Bethel, Dr. J. Wallace Hamilton, Dr. Stanley Shoemaker, Dr. S. Marion Smith, Dr. Kenneth Wheeler, Jack Haskins, Philip Crosby, et al.

Prologue
Sanity

She jumped out of the bushes at me. I was 25 years old, working on my doctorate in Indianapolis, and had just started a year's training of Clinical Pastoral Education at Central State Hospital for the mentally insane. (That was the term they used back in those days.)

The place was downright scary. It was not merely that I had watched way too many horror movies. It was also that I had come from a small town in Ohio where the tallest building was a grain elevator and the biggest risk was hitting a skunk with your car. I was not ready for this.

That day, with no traffic directors on the grounds, no signs pointing me to the right building, no greeters or ushers in place for visitors, I wandered toward a foreboding Gothic building. It appeared to be empty. As I stepped into its open courtyard, a flock of pigeons burst into the air. My heart shot blood into my brain, now experiencing combined flashbacks of Hitchcock's horror movies *The Birds* and *Psycho*.

Looking around for any hint of an administration building, I saw a more contemporary-style brick building. I turned toward it and disciplined myself to walk confidently, as if I were a professional health-care worker. Inside I was saying, "God, don't let the birds peck me to death or the crazy people get me!" But outside, I was very dignified, so far.

As I was walking toward what I thought was the administration building, a little parade of patients was being led across campus. As they passed by, I noticed that most of them showed signs of being sedated. Their attendants were talking among themselves instead of watching the group.

The brick building was not administration. The room to which I was to report was back the way I had come. So I started my return journey. The weather was bleak, almost foggy. The campus was silent. There was a little building to the left surrounded by bushes that looked like giant balls of tumbleweed.

I was only a few yards from that building when a woman jumped from the bushes to confront me. She had been in the parade; she had waited for me to return. Her hair was unkempt; the coat she was wearing might have been someone else's because it covered her slippers.

Her eyes narrowed and she shouted at me, "I know who you are and what you have been saying about me! And if you don't stop, I WILL KILL YOU!" Then she just walked away. I could have sworn I heard her humming a hymn. Whatever it was that she was humming, I could tell that our encounter had not had the same effect on her that it had on me.

I could not stop thinking about that moment, or her words, until I could come up with some sort of explanation. I needed to analyze the encounter to deal with my own sense of trauma. And more important, I needed to learn a lesson from an unexpected teacher. There was something about her that captivated my heart. I felt compassion for her, and I felt compelled to understand the reason for her outburst.

It didn't take me long. As I thought through that confrontation, I recognized instinctively a reason for her separation and anger.

It was not social; it was antisocial. She was not responding to me. We had never met. She was responding to the voices in her own head. She had not heard real outside voices accusing me, only her own inner voices assuming malice on the outside. She was trapped within herself. She thought she was relating to the real world, but her perceptions were limited to her own personal world. That is a good definition of insanity and a good reason for pity.

People living within a world limited to their own perspectives cannot expect to be loving or accurate in response to "outsiders." Insanity is being trapped within yourself.

The church has grown more and more isolated over the years as it has withdrawn more and more into itself. If postmodernity can be partially defined as a resignation to the limitations of one's own perspective, if the church does not have genuine communication with the rest of the world (outsiders), if Christians are suspicious that the very people God sends to help are enemies, then *aren't we insane*?

That kind of isolation in the church started with its institutionalization after the conversion of Emperor Constantine in A.D. 312. Given the power to distance itself from the attacks from outside, and to jettison disagreements on the inside, the church began building walls. The fearful suspicion due to separation increased, and its mental conditions were passed on with the hardening of the denominational boundaries following the Reformation in the early 1500s. Institutionalized, the church finally rested in the current heresy (heresy is not untruth; it is focusing on part of the truth as if it were the main truth) of church organizations that believe churches to be fundamentally separate entities.

Most churches trod on hellishly alone …

Introduction
A Relational and Rational Way of Doing Church

So what is the distributed church, anyway? It's a church that isn't insane. It is able to pay attention to and learn from outsiders. It is a way to be completed, perfected and educated by differences. Linking complementary Christians together for long-term support and effective ministry, church arranged like this participates more fully in the sovereignty of God.

This is not another church-growth strategy or some let's-play-nice-together ecumenical effort. It is a connecting strategy that results in spiritual maturity. Connecting the church is the means, *not* the goal. Christ came so that people could be saved. He poured His life out for those outside the Kingdom. The world needs Christ, and Christians must intentionally combine in more effective ways to go into the world to present the Gospel and support each other for the harvest.

Virtually any church in any denomination can become a church distributed. Formed for practical partnerships, not theological details, distributed church partnerships can take place inside, outside or across denominational boundaries. The distributed model works in tandem with church-growth plans. Just getting bigger isn't good enough; we have got to get better! Greater depth results from greater breadth. Deeply committed to God, we can accomplish more *because of our differences*—without giving up our unique identities—than we can accomplish on our own.

In the present model of the church, the local church tends to be isolated and preoccupied with its own world. It appears to be, and often is, self-centered. Our triune God, by His very nature, models relationship-centeredness. God in Christ came out of His self-sufficiency to identify with those radically different from Himself, and His church is called to be like Him. The church that is distributed values ministry beyond its walls more than ministry inside them because it focuses on those not yet included. It reaches through relationships it has within its congregation to identify with others. Intentional distribution of the church with a goal of ultimate connection through relationship reflects God's image.

Christian, wake up: YOU ARE A MINISTER OF THE CHURCH. You don't need to know more; you don't need to have a church program commission you—although both can be useful. But you need to understand that in this definition of the church that you *are* a minister of the church and you can further ministry by connecting with other believers who are different from yourself.

People in Northland's congregation take leadership of nearly every ministry effort inside the church, out in the community and abroad. Elders, pastors and paid staff have a hand-off approach— they literally hand off the ministry God has given a person, to that Spirit-led person! They don't try to control the initiatives of congregants or the connections they make, and they don't watch over their shoulders unnecessarily. Elders, pastors and paid staff pray for them, get them the training and resources they need, and if someone's doing something weird or flaky, the church leaders hear about it and follow up. But there is no doubt in anyone's mind that we all are on the same team.

This is freeing not just for congregants, it's freeing for leaders because they don't have to be everywhere trying to run everything. And as you might imagine, much more ministry gets done when procedures and systems aren't esteemed over service. I always encourage those who worship at Northland: "Do what you can, where you are, with what you've got." And they do!

We are simply following the pattern set in the early church. Since the earliest times, God has distributed His spiritual gifts (1 Corinthians 12:7, 11) so that each person is of value to others and all are dependent on one another for the fulfillment of their mission together (1 Corinthians 12:20-21). It is through the distribution of these gifts that God creates both the personalized extension of His Spirit and the unity of His church.

For centuries, the church has distributed Christians into the world to fulfill their callings and has kept building relationships based on their service to others. Acts 13:1-3 gives an account of God initiating a call on particular individuals and the church sending (distributing) them to a ministry that will later result in relationships for that church. As the movement builds, specific territories are put in the hearts of the sent ones (Acts 16:9-10) resulting in a network of churches sharing resources to better help people (2 Corinthians 8:1-5). The Bible speaks of "the church ... which is at ... with all ... in every place" (see 1 Corinthians 1:2). The early church, the New Testament Church, was a church distributed.

God designed us to work in partnership. Multi-agent partnerships are distributed systems. In fact, most of nature— and most of technology—are distributed systems. On a macro level, every ecosystem is a distributed system because each one has interdependent and widely varied components. If even one component of the functional unit we call an ecosystem fails, then everything in that system is affected. On the micro level, the smallest entities of the universe all have interrelated connections. When an elementary particle, the photon, is stimulated an immediate response can be detected in a photon eight miles away. There is no doubt that the universe is connected.

Survival in ever-changing environments requires interaction with others. Integration of differences is a key to a hardy life—even in the plant world. As any botanist will attest, the simplest form of replication for a plant is self-pollenization, but there is a problem with that. The singular set of genes gave the plant characteristics to suit it perfectly for one specific set of environmental circumstances, but its hardiness lies within those narrow parameters. Defined only by its own previous generations of DNA, it will die if there is much change in its circumstances. To get a much hardier plant, one that is able to thrive in a changing environment, cross-pollenization is key. The genetic code of more than one parent plant is required for the best chance at a hardy plantlet. A certain level of strength and health is gained only through relationships with outsiders and that isn't just true for plants.

The church, at large, is missing a way to benefit from differences, and that is affecting its strength and health. Fear and suspicion of differences limit the church's spiritual maturity. Both spiritual and intellectual maturity grow from differences. A distributed church uses contrasts to accomplish Kingdom purposes.

I See That Hand

Already have questions about the distributed church that will be distracting you until they are answered? Since I have no way of knowing what your questions are at this point, I'll just interject a brief Q&A that might be helpful in setting a context for you before we get to Chapter One (more FAQs can be found at the end of the book).

What is the definition of the distributed church?

The definition is multifold and will be unpacked as we go along. But in summary, a church distributed is a church turned inside out. It is a church that values and makes the most of differences in the Body of Christ and works through outside relationships, not just inside programs. It places the resources of the church close to people rather than asking people to come to the resources. Multisite worship can be part of becoming a distributed church, but there's more to it than that. Again, a definition will reveal itself as the book unfolds.

Why is it important that we structure the church to reflect the nature of our triune God?

Every structure has an effect on the thinking and function of what it houses. If we arrange the church with a hierarchy—like a government or a business or the traditional church—it will operate like those institutions. The more we make the basis of the church interdependent relationships the more our thinking and function will reflect the nature of our triune God (2 Corinthians 3:18). That's why the distributed church has a structure that reflects the nature of God, who is within Himself a relationship.

What should be the central orienting activities of the church?

As Jesus summarized the law in Matthew 22:37-41, our first activity is to love God (worship) and then to love our neighbor (service). Pretty simple, but you would be surprised what can get in the way of those two priorities. Our Christian response to Jesus' imperative is to love God and our neighbor. That means prioritizing and living a life of worship and service. That's why the distributed church has as its central orienting activities, worship and service, and equipping people for those two lifestyles.

Why are most local churches homogeneous in makeup?

They are affinity-based and limited by a perspective that says,

"You have to stay narrow to 'go deep' with God." The distributed church believes that going broad is the only way to truly go deep with God. I'm reminded of a well digger's comment, "Once you hit water you stop digging and share what you've found." Engagement with people and ideas that are different from our own are potentially intimidating and almost always uncomfortable. But we can gain spiritual and intellectual maturity when dissimilar people are a necessary part of a congregation. Linking differences and bridging distances for the benefit of all is a key element of the church distributed. A heterogeneous makeup is a natural result of those efforts

What can cause the undoing of the institutional church?

It starts out to get people saved and equip them for service. It proceeds by serving people who come inside a building. Then it settles for elevating the programs and obligations of the gathered congregation until, finally, the costs exceed the benefits to those who attend. Meanwhile, the church virtually forgets about the world outside. If the church exists to include those not yet included in heaven, and those not yet included are to know we are Christians by our love, we need to be based in geographical proximity to them. That's why the church distributed plan is field-based, not headquarters-based.

What makes the church grow?

We may assume that the church grows by acquisition, accumulation, and assimilation rather than by affiliation. Wrong assumption. Both groups and individuals grow more distinct and effective by the partnerships they develop. As an individual, I am made to have a relational identity. I am made to include differences that transform "me" into "us."

In the garden, when God called to the man, "Where are you?" the question was not mainly geographical. It was biographical. It was the observation of a painful separation that then characterized the relationship. It was a way to note the searching of God and the isolation of man. Later, entire groups would be characterized by their isolation. That's why the distributed church chooses to grow by connection, not by accumulation.

Many of your questions about the distributed church will be answered in these pages, but if you accept the challenge of being part of it, you might as well know now that the distributed church will be partially defined by your life of worship and service.

One of the main reasons I have written this book is to encourage individuals (you) and congregations: It is time to connect, grow and go.

Summary Prayer
Lord, take me from where You have been in my life to where You are waiting for me in theirs. Amen.

dis•trib´•ut•ed church (di-strib-yoo-tid chûrch)
noun

- A church that centers on God and revolves around
  others rather than insisting that "our church" is
  the center of the universe. This is a "Copernican
  Revolution" of the church.

ONE
It's Personal
From 'Disturbed' to Distributed

I love the church. I have loved the church since Gran first took me there when I was a little boy. We had the same routine every week. My sister and I would stay at Gran and Pop's house on Saturday nights. We would watch Lawrence Welk on television and sometimes we would play a card game called Canasta. Gran had a turn-the-crank card shuffler, which was a pretty worldly investment for an old-time Methodist. After the game, I would watch the *Gillette Saturday Night Fights* with Pop.

"Who are we rooting for?" I'd ask.

"That guy on the right," he'd say.

"Why him?"

"'Cause he's the underdog," Pop would say. "We always root for the underdog, Joey."

I could never tell if we were rooting for the underdog because Pop was a Democrat or because he wanted to see those who were "high and mighty" knocked down a peg or two. The latter was one of the reasons that Pop didn't go to church.

On Sunday morning, we went to church with Gran. Pop always stayed home. "I'll watch the roast so it won't burn," he'd say. Sometimes he'd mumble something about hypocrites, but I didn't know what that was. I thought maybe he was just having trouble bending his knees, which turned out to be the case.

First Methodist Church, Shelby, Ohio, was a wondrous place. With rich, dark wood and wine-colored carpet, the sanctuary was sobering. There was a stained glass window with Jesus in it. That added a little color. But Jesus was in the Garden of Gethsemane, so even that was somber.

In those days, people dressed up for church in their best clothes. Ladies wore hats with plastic fruit attached, and men wore pinstripes on their suits. Dr. Shoemaker, our minister, wore a long, flowing robe and was distinguished in presence and speech. He used words too big for me to understand, but somehow I knew they were important.

Gran always had to sit in the third pew from the back on the left side, behind Mrs. Price, who always wore purple. If some "visitor" accidentally sat in her pew, Gran just couldn't worship right. But she never said anything mean on those rare occasions, what with her being a Christian and all.

When I grew restless, Gran would slip me a butterscotch candy. I would spend a long time trying to unwrap that candy without making a sound. It was impolite to make noise in church, especially sounds caused by unwrapping candy. It was okay to cough quietly, though, so if I wanted to make big strides in the unwrapping, I would coordinate it with a cough. Finally, I would get that candy in my mouth. I loved butterscotch, but that wasn't the best part.

After I got the wrapper separate from the candy, I would hold that yellow cellophane stretched between my hands and place it in front of one of my eyes. Then, I would close the other eye and look around the sanctuary through the cellophane. The entire sanctuary instantly went from a dark, foreboding place to a sunshine-filled space.

Years later, when I finally learned that Christ's sacrifice on the cross made me appear righteous to God, it was not difficult for me to understand. I just pictured God picking up the cross and looking through it at my life, so dark with sin, and saying, "You look good to Me, Joel … like My son."

Today, I still love the church. I want to see it extended. Millions find their way to the same pews every Sunday, but there are billions who do not. There are millions who have family to take them to church, so they will associate it with God's love (even if it is boring or separated from everyday life). But there are increasing billions who do not have someone who cares, and they have no connection to the church at all.

That is why I don't want to see the church enclosed and self-limiting. The church is the main venue for the hope of the world; it just cannot seem to penetrate the very world that needs it.

Alone Together

When my grandmother took my sister and me to worship every Sunday, the church was filled with reverence, mystery and a distinct sense of the presence of God. Unfortunately, that sense evaporated quickly once we were outside its doors. I could not wait to take off my tie and get back to "regular life." I could not imagine God having anything to do with football, bullies or girls. I missed Him when I was not in church.

The church was its own world. I remember my surprise when I once saw our young associate pastor at our athletic field. He was practicing the discus throw. He had on shorts and a cut-off shirt, and it seemed to me that he could throw that discus a country mile. All of the high school athletes around him were using profane language to vent frustration about their errant throws. I warned as many as I could that the guy right over there was a minister, but I thought the whole situation was just a bad fit. What was a minister doing in our world, anyway? It never occurred to me that I, too, was a representative of that church living in that profane world every day. After all, the church was its own world.

I loved the church when I was a boy, and I have loved the church since I was a young pastor of a small congregation in southern Indiana. That integrated congregation was a merger of three little congregations: a country-dwellers church, a retired blue-collar-workers church and an African-American church. But in most ways, we were as isolated from other churches as church life was from the real world.

Church members used to tell me: "We aren't like other churches in our denomination, preacher. We aren't like First Church. They've got a big choir and a lot of upper-class people. We aren't like the Baptists or the Pentecostals either; we are quieter. We aren't like the Presbyterians—you know the old joke, God elected them, but we had to find Him on our own. We're just folks."

We had an eighty-year-old organist who bragged, "I never had a lesson in my life." She was so conscientious … and so tired. Sometimes she fell asleep at the organ while I was preaching and her foot would slip and hit a pedal. The loud "honk" would startle her and several others. But she was all we had; at least that's what we thought.

Our choir was just as memorable. It had just two men. Frank was a marvelous singer who in his younger days was offered a scholarship to the Chicago Conservatory of Music. But because he had a job in a gas station, and that was such a good job for a black youth in those days, he decided not to go to Chicago.

The only other man in our choir was Alva, the saw sharpener.

Alva was a wonderful man, one of the kindest men I've ever had the privilege to know. Oblivious to the fact that he wasn't the greatest singer in the world, he sang out loudly, loving the idea that he was helping the choir. The congregation just tried to hear Frank instead of Alva. It was a charming and endearing church-family matter. They were all we had; at least that's what we thought.

Not so charming was a woman who had been the Sunday school superintendent for thirty years because no one else would do it. She was tired and bitter. But, we all thought she was all we had. It was not charming, either, that only three kids and an untrained leader came to youth group. But we all thought that these were all we had.

There were other churches around us that were large enough to have people who could have relieved the organist, supplemented the men in the choir, let the superintendent off for a season. Other churches could have welcomed our youth into a larger, more spiritually maturing youth group without "stealing" them. But it was understood: "Our church is different from other churches, preacher." So we just stayed by ourselves.

Later, I became the pastor of a large and fast-growing denominational church. It had grown from 200 worshipers to almost 1,000 in worship. We needed more land and wanted to move. But we were forbidden by the denomination because the land that we had been offered by a church member encroached upon the "territory" of another church in our denomination. The denomination's refusal to grant permission was okay. We understood.

But what was not okay was the disconnection I felt within a supposedly connected denomination. Other ministers I talked to felt it too. How could the very togetherness of being in a denomination with a common mission not bring fellowship and a way to work together? What were we missing?

The Wake-Up Call

At 37, I thought I would be serving that denominational church forever; then something very strange happened. In the middle of the night, I awoke out of a sound sleep. I sat straight up in bed. My heart was racing. I immediately got up and began walking around the room. My wife woke up and asked, "What's wrong?"

"I don't know," I said. "My heart is just all disturbed."

"Like a heart attack?"

"No, it's not like a physical problem."

"Bad dream?"

"I don't know. I can't remember dreaming anything."

Eventually, I went back to bed. I slept soundly for the rest of the night. But the next night the same thing happened. I woke up out of a sound sleep with my heart disturbed. The next night it happened, too. And the next …

Eventually, I went away for a time of prayer and fasting. Through a series of thoughts and a sign, God let me know that we would be moving. He just didn't say where or when.

I went home to tell Becky. I was not sure how she would take the news. After fifteen years in ministry, we had no money in the bank. The denomination owned our house and held our insurance. We had three small boys and one old car. We would be walking away from every known form of security. But when I told Becky what I thought I had heard, her response was immediate: "Give me two days to pack," she said. "I'll follow you anywhere." I will always be grateful for that.

After an extended process of praying and searching, we interviewed with a struggling church in Orlando. They had just bought an old, dilapidated roller skating rink to make into a church. They had recently gone through a church split, and some of them were wondering whether God would even have them stay together as a church.

Their search process, though, was extensive and exact. We had conversation after conversation. By the end of the process, they knew more about me than anyone had ever cared to ask. I remember thinking, "These people are so competent. I would love to work with them."

It became evident to Becky and me that this congregation was our future family. It was only after they had chosen us that I realized why it felt so right for all of us. In a conversation with Becky, an elder's wife said, "We want you to know, you are an answer to our prayers."

Becky responded immediately, "And you are an answer to ours."

The elder's wife, however, wanted us to know the deeper story. "No, I mean literally—you are a direct answer to our prayers. Months ago, a small group of us women began to meet together and pray that God would disturb the heart of the pastor who was supposed to be here."

A shiver went through Becky. "When did you begin to pray that?" Of course, their prayer was initiated at the same time I began to sit straight up in bed, night after night, with my heart disturbed. Over a span of a thousand miles, God had connected us. That personal call, which came to us from a church we knew nothing about, began our sense of the church that is distributed yet not separated.

However, in one sense, the church to which God had connected us was immature. I mean that in the middle-school-age sense. Northland Community Church defined itself by the kind of church it was not. If the traditional church did something, Northland did not want to do it. Traditional churches had beautiful buildings and choirs and committees and formality. Northland wanted no part of it.

Though the strategy of being different was understandable, the church had developed an attitude of rebellion and reverse pride. Like an adolescent who defines himself by what he hates, Northland, like many churches, got stuck in a negative identity. A negative-identity church prides itself on what it is not but can't really describe what it is in positive terms. That kind of negative identity kept us distant from other churches.

God continued to demonstrate countless and awesome acts of grace in and through the church. We had a great leadership team, a congregation any pastor would love to serve, and a shining future. Yet we had that same problem as in my previous church, and the one before that, and the one before that: We were doing ministry alone. We were isolated from other churches in our efforts as individuals and as a congregation.

Something needed to change ...

CONCEPTS IN CONTEXT
You, Christian, are a minister of the church.

Here are three challenges to help you personalize ideas found in Chapter One.

1. Move from "disturbed" to distributed: Stop thinking about what you want and think about what might be best for everyone in your home, church, workplace or the community at large. If symptoms of selfishness reappear, repeat above.

2. Hear the wake-up call: Carve some time out of your daily routine to spend time with God. Block a day on your calendar to spend with Him and make the necessary arrangements that will allow you to do it.

3. Conquer "alone-together" life: Contact a church, or an individual Christian or an organization with Christian values that is striving to serve others and ask them how you can help them accomplish their ministry goals. Then do something, even if it is a little thing, to support them in their ministry.

dis•trib´•ut•ed church (di-strib-yoo-tid chûrch)

noun

- A church that centers on God and revolves around others rather than insisting that "our church" is the center of the universe. This is a "Copernican Revolution" of the church.

verb

- Putting the resources of the church as close to people as possible, offering meeting points and access to resources, in order to assist Christians in helping others.

TWO
A Church for Others

In 1988, three years after I arrived at Northland, we finished a construction project that made our building, an old roller rink, look presentable. Prior to my arrival, the recently purchased rink had not been used for some time, and it was a mess. For several years, it was less a church than a construction site. Finally, the couple hundred hearty souls, who had so faithfully made their way between the dumpsters to come to worship, completed the building upgrade.

A year later, I had a nagging sense that God had a plan for us as a congregation. Being the busy pastor of a growing church, I tried to listen, but kept putting Him on hold as the duties of daily life called for my time. So the elders sent me away to spend time alone with God and told me to come back only when I thought I understood what God was desiring for the church.

During that two-week retreat I became convinced that God wanted me to preach on one theme per year for ten years. Consistent focus on one area of the faith would build spiritual maturity by weaving biblical themes into our character rather than just inserting scriptural principles into our short-term memories. And, it would keep us together on a common and focused journey for a sustained period of time.

During that ten-year preaching series, we were growing in worship attendance at a rapid rate. The attendance figures went from 300 to well over 5,000. The staff grew from four to ninety; the budget grew from a few hundred thousand dollars to eight million; we went from one service on Sunday morning to seven services throughout the weekend. We then faced building limitations so severe that the attendance reached a plateau at around 6,000.

The growth of Northland forced us to make a decision as to the future character of our church. We obviously had grown big enough to become a society within a society. If we had wanted to just do the traditional things to accommodate growth (i.e. be in perennial building programs, pressure people to volunteer in the church, encourage people to live as much of their lives at the church building as possible), then we could probably have kept growing. But growing what—another mega-church? Would we be promoting the unspoken message that our congregation was more important to us or—even worse—to God, than other congregations and ministries? Would we be furthering the Western mentality of the rugged individualism of a church, while ignoring the larger community life of the church (a philosophy that is neither biblical nor appropriate)? These concerns remained on the table for discussion for weeks. Then one Sunday, a woman who was part of our prayer ministry team brought me a present: a cross-stitch that she had designed to highlight something I had mentioned in a sermon the first month I preached at Northland. To this day her handiwork sits on a shelf near my desk to remind me, "Northland, Just One of God's Churches." That sentiment is a thread woven through our vision and mission.

Toward the end of that ten-year *Journey Toward Spiritual Maturity* preaching schedule, I presented to the elders a vision I had about a new way of doing church. They decided to do something radical

("radical" means "from the roots").

The elders, after prayer and debate, decided to change our church's course from a local "community church" to "a church distributed." The elders' decision to change the understanding of Northland from a community church to a distributed church was anything but easy or instant. That decision was made at a retreat for the pastors, elders and their wives. The elders were "big picture" and "long-term" thinkers, so the discussion among us was more than lively. To begin the retreat, we put sheets of paper along the wall and traced the spiritual history of Northland. Since our church was only about 25 years old at the time, it was easy for most of the leaders to collaborate and remember the high and low points. In addition, that same timeline filled quickly with their personal points of spiritual growth. Each one marked the date they joined the church and many indicated the highs and lows in their personal faith journeys.

Then I spoke for about an hour, proposing a greatly expanded view, not just of Northland, but of the local-church paradigm itself. A good local church could be said to be a truly "community" church. Years ago, thousands of churches began to put "Community Church" into their names because they had the desire to minister to those who came to the church and to those living nearby who might. There was no risk in the name (other than minimizing a denominational affiliation). The Community Church was simply a contemporary expression of the old parish system: church at the center of a geographical area, and an expectation that everyone who lived near it should come to it. The problem was that lots of the denominational or independent churches wanted to be the spiritual center of the same geographical area. While community churches multiplied, mega-churches that drew from an entire region also started popping up. These mega-churches, including Northland, drew from many surrounding communities. Was it still accurate to be labeled a "community church"? To make matters even more complicated, globalization was becoming a reality that would affect the future of many mega-churches. The traditional terms of "mega-church," "community church," even "missional church" all pointed to confined entities that had focused target groups.

The new proposal: Northland should continue growing by serving and connecting to outsiders where they are, rather than getting them to join us. Those outsiders should be linked through relationships that God is already building rather than by planned objectives set by a mission board. Resources and empowerment for service should flow outward instead of inward. And the church should see itself located in many places instead of one place. In 1996, church was a gathered congregation; church as a multi-agent network was a new and mostly untested concept. That a church building would be secondary, or someday largely unnecessary for most of the congregation was not a common way of thinking.

There was very little hostility in the room, just very intense prayer and searching for what this might mean. The problem was, I could not explain it, because I did not know what it would mean! As the retreat came to a close, one pastor was going to quit and some of the leaders had serious reservations, but everyone gathered around me and prayed for Northland. As they laid hands on me and placed their confidence in the thought that God was leading us in this new direction, I felt a relief and an excitement I can say I had never felt before. I also felt a reverent fear.

In a congregational meeting later, several people expressed confusion and anger about changing the name of the church. Because the concept was so new to us, we could not give them enough clarity to quell their frustration. That was a problem. But we had a consensus in the leadership that God was calling us to do something wider and deeper than our past version of a community church with a mission program. The details of that calling were still a mystery.

For three years after that decision we were still wrestling with what it means to have some of our deepest relationships be with congregations and Christian ministries beyond Northland's walls. What does it mean to be defined as a congregation in the context of outside relationships? Some church-family members were fearful: "Does this mean that we can no longer be as close to each other as a congregation?" Others asked, "Shouldn't we be spending our time building and perfecting community here before we 'export' ourselves?"

At a loss to explain something that was not yet evident, we watched as God started to put into place what we, as a church body, could not yet conceptualize.

Our First Partner

It happened when Northland's pastors and elders from Florida were helping ordain the new pastor of Christ Church in Amherst, New Hampshire, a nondenominational church of hundreds of intelligent and devoted believers. "If it weren't for your church, our church probably would not be around right now," one of their elders said to our elder board chairman. Though our churches were a thousand miles apart in geography, and far apart in experience, we had so much in common. We knew we were going to be working together for a long time.

Two years prior to that ordination service, a leader from Christ Church had visited Northland. While speaking with one of the pastors, he mentioned that his church had just lost its pastor. He went on to say how discouraged they were, even to the point of wondering if it was time to disband as a church. Then, half-joking, he said, "You have so many pastors here, why don't you send us one? At least to preach for a while!"

When that comment was repeated among the pastors, we laughed ... at first. Then we thought together, "We do have plenty of leaders here who might love the chance to help a small church over a rough time."

A little calculation proved it would actually cost less for that New Hampshire church to fly one of our pastors there and pay him a small honorarium to preach than to pay a full-time pastor. If the New Hampshire congregation did decide to look for a new pastor, such a temporary pastoral supply might have several benefits.

This temporary arrangement would relieve them of the time and financial pressure of having to hire a new pastor right away. A nondenominational congregation with strong lay leadership, they could survive without a full-time pastor for quite a while if they knew the preaching was covered. Asking a larger congregation's help in finding the right pastor for them made perfect sense.

Initially, my son Isaac, a seminary student, flew there every weekend to preach. The church loved the idea of helping to shape and encourage a young man in the beginning years of his ministry. He received experience in preaching and a taste of life in a smaller congregation.

After some months, other pastors from our staff got involved too. Since I did most of the preaching at our church, this provided them more preaching experience, plus a little extra income.

The greatest thrill for both churches, though, was the thought of working together. Through the many conversations and visits between leaders, relationships were beginning to develop. Neither congregation had ever been convinced that the best way to do ministry was to do it alone. We wanted the genuine unity that

Christ had prayed for (John 17:20-23). We wanted to have "family" in other places.

For nearly two years, Northland Church in Orlando, Florida, sent preachers to Christ Church in Amherst, New Hampshire, almost every weekend. That is what the first-century church did: They sent leadership back and forth because they saw themselves as one church family located in different places.

Next Steps

But sharing leadership was just part of our vision as a distributed church. We also wanted to put the resources of the church close to where our congregants live. That way, they could connect with neighboring Christians for support and encouragement and better serve their communities.

In our first attempt to distribute the church into the community, we began to build Neighborhood Networks. The goal was to take the resources and support systems to medium-sized sections of the congregation (30-300 people) and move the center of church life nearer to their homes. We wanted people to have the presence and support of the church near their homes, integrated into "real life."

These Neighborhood Networks, the larger gatherings of our small-group ministry, found places to meet in their own part of the community. Some met in civic halls or larger homes. Some rented local church fellowship halls. As a result, we developed wonderful relationships with church leaders throughout Central Florida.

That first attempt at distributing Northland into the many different geographical locations where our church family actually lived, provided a number of advantages and services that the congregation-at-a-single-place usually cannot offer, including a close-to-home place to serve and an alternative to driving back to the church building every time someone needed to be connected with the church.

I keep using past tense verbs, however, because Neighborhood Networks was not a long-term solution.

In "autopsy" discussions, it was determined that the ultimate cause of death for this first attempt at distributed sites was a lack of concurrent worship. Since our congregation has always centered its life and direction from worship together, the Neighborhood Networks eventually began to feel like additional meetings rather than the core of our church expression. We would begin to remedy that.

Our First Distributed Site

With the benefits of the Neighborhood Networks still in mind, we knew we were on to the right philosophy, even if we had not perfected the model.

The traditional church assumes that the ideal for togetherness is getting all of a local congregation into one worship service, at one place. But such a setting does not impress upon the worshipers how large and varied and powerful God's family is. The problems with trying to cram into one building for seven worship services each weekend were numerous:

1. We had no room for adult or middle/high Sunday school at worship times.
2. We had to settle for large-group children's activities rather than smaller, more individualized classes.
3. We had virtually no room for growth in worship services (our sanctuary capacity was 1,200, and our average weekend attendance was around 6,500).

4. We had lacked the space to launch new initiatives for a long time; the creative people were getting stagnant.

We took the next step toward becoming a distributed church in the midst of coping with these practical problems.

In 2001, for a while after the 9/11 attack by Islamic extremists, the churches in America were overflowing. Northland was one of those churches with significantly increased attendance, and we had to find additional worship space immediately. Because we had a good relationship with a high school just down the street, we asked if we could use the new auditorium that they had just built. We would need it only on Sunday mornings (at least initially), and we were willing to sign up for a six-month trial period. They let us know that the great relationship one of our pastors had established with their school administrators over the years, and the fact that Northland had served the school by offering our facilities to meet their space needs in the past, made their decision easy. They decided to rent us space.

Through the use of technology, in addition to overcoming space limitations, it was so exciting for our local congregation to worship together in two places at once! Concurrent worship erased the distance between our two locations. Able to see each other on the screens, we had solved, rather inexpensively, the other practical problem. Some other churches in the U.S. had already started to go to multiple campuses, and we soon joined a consortium of multi-site churches. Our initial sites were purposed around concurrent worship. Reflecting God's singular-and-plural-at-once being was the overarching principle. Trinitarian theology was being demonstrated by our worship arrangement.

We began by worshiping concurrently in two of our Sunday morning services. The first few Sundays there were 500; then there were 600; and soon 700 were attending those two services at Lyman

High School in addition to the 1,200 seated in the original Northland sanctuary. At first, Lyman housed only worship and childcare for the youngest children. Two months into the new site's service, however, Sunday school for children and adults was added.

The worship services began with T1 phone line hook-ups for video and audio capabilities. Then, because of the geographical proximity, we laid fiber-optic cable between the two worship sites, enabling us to worship interactively in real time. We have responsive readings, duets, and other types of worship leadership exchanges between the two sites. There is truly a feeling of togetherness. On occasion, I start my sermon at one location, only to finish it at another. Some people think I have a twin.

In 2007, this congregation of 12,000 now worships every weekend at several sites throughout Central Florida. The concurrent worship experience extends spiritual vision with an awareness of how many other brothers and sisters in Christ are worshiping God as we are. It is a powerful expansion of worship! It is powerful not only because we can see each other and feel connected, but also because the need for connection is hardwired into our spirits.

In addition to our weekly connections with our multiple Florida sites, about 1,500 sites connect every weekend via Northland's Webstream Worship online. It is important to note that those who join us for worship via the Webstream are participating in the service. Many are hosting small groups in their homes and have "home church" with Northland. We often receive an email request at the church for study materials from an online worshiper who has accepted the invitation to receive Christ as their personal Lord and Savior. Such requests have come from a diverse range of people and places: a patient in a local hospital as well as a teacher thousands of miles away in another country, and hundreds of people in between, have discovered a personal relationship with Jesus Christ through participation in online worship services. Northland's prayer team often receives prayer requests from those joining us online, and most Webstream worshipers celebrate with us in bringing their tithes and offerings via online giving. While most churches try to draw people in from miles away, a distributed church ministers to people right where they live.

Our linking is not merely one-way information masquerading as relationship; it is mutual expansion and capability by connection. There is an analogy of this form of church in Richard Shaffer's explanation of linked computers:

> "In these networked days, the real power of a computer is less in the machine itself than in the combined power of all the other computers to which it is connected ... the network is the computer."[1]

Multi-site concurrent worship and online worship are just part of our journey as a church distributed. We are constantly reorienting our ministry efforts from inside to outside, from solitary to partnered, to an arrangement that consistently reminds us of God.

There is a very practical reason for this ...

CONCEPTS IN CONTEXT
You, Christian, are a minister of the church.

Here are three challenges to help you personalize ideas found in Chapter Two.

1) Build a church for others: Discover what relationships members of your local church already have with those who are not part of that congregation. See if there are ways you can expand on any of those relationships. For example, does someone have a friend in another country? Has someone at the church "adopted" a

Compassion Child (www.compassion.com) halfway around the world? Investigate taking a small group from your church into the neighborhood where that friend or child lives to learn about his life and to discover ways you can help him and those in his spheres of influence to love Jesus more. If the global thing sounds like a bit bigger step than you were thinking of taking right away, consider expanding on a relationship that is already growing in your community. Is someone in your church helping out a single mother by watching her kids after school so she can complete her day's work? Is there a small group, or class in your church that would be willing to "adopt her family" and love on them in ways that go way beyond child care? If someone registers her kids for a baseball team or swimming lessons and goes and cheers them on, ministry happens not just with the child and that family, but also in the connections that are made in the bleachers. Believers do such things because they see all of life as ministry. The church is built for others.

2) Take steps with a partner: Consider for a moment who God has put in your life that you enjoy—individuals or groups that share your biblical values, bring out the best in you, and from whom you gain as much as you give. Ask if you two could partner in a specific project to help others. You will both make much greater ministry progress than you could alone. The best partnerships are bonded by united effort in the same direction.

3) Choose a distributed site: Worship with friends in a setting you prefer. Invite those you know who are homebound, or traveling. Ask those who are trying to be "salt and light" in a discouraged local church, or those who have sworn, "I will never step into another church," to participate in live worship services via Internet technology. This is an option numerous churches, including Northland, have already made available, and more

churches will offer it with each coming year. You can Google *live worship services* and you will discover a wide range of worship styles to choose from. Christians all worship the triune God so select a worship service that helps you best honor Him. Of course, you are always welcome to worship with Northland via Webstream any weekend at www.northlandchurch.net. We'd love to have you.

dis•trib´•ut•ed church (di-strib-yoo-tid chûrch)

noun

- A church that centers on God and revolves around others rather than insisting that "our church" is the center of the universe. This is a "Copernican Revolution" of the church.

verb

- Putting the resources of the church as close to people as possible, offering meeting points and access to resources, in order to assist Christians in helping others.
- Connecting to outsiders and serving them where they are, rather than getting them to join us.

THREE
A Church for Tomorrow

A pilot without a plane is called a pedestrian. A coach without a team is called a fan. A business without a delivery system is called a warehouse. A gathering of Christians without a way to link with other ministries is called a local church. We cannot fulfill our potential without an appropriate vehicle of transport beyond ourselves.

Traditional Christians probably do not realize the term "local church" is almost synonymous with the word "island." Most local churches have become so preoccupied with catering to the needs of those who meet in the church building that they have forgotten the potential of love. Like the faithful but self-righteous elder brother in the prodigal son story (Luke 15:11-32), groups focusing too much on their own territorial accomplishments will miss the greater celebration. We will miss so much if we limit our exuberance to what happens within the walls we've built.

Our knowledge, skill, character, potential and even our personal contribution will not be fully accomplished without others. *As iron sharpens iron, so one man sharpens another* (Proverbs 27:17). The completion of our goals and achievement of our potential require interaction.

The distributed church is designed to transcend postmodern times. The arrangement of the centuries-old local-church-with-a-mission-program is too categorical to be responsive and relational in a culture of rapid change and dispersion of community. Some of the new expressions of the church are wonderful, and corrective of the shortcomings of the traditional structure. The "missional" and "emerging" churches, for example, are terrific ways of doing church. I can see the benefits of both.

The "emerging church" has arisen in the last couple of decades to unclasp its congregants from the more mechanical and categorized traditions of the church. It values the creativity of its adherents and seeks to more personally shape their lives specifically and authentically like the life of Jesus. That's great!

The "missional church" prioritizes the reforming of the church to more fully and completely engage the surrounding non-Christian culture. It truly wants to be "salt and light" fully embedded in the world, so it avoids the "Christianese" terms and stylized forms of worship and prayers. At the same time, it seeks to live a distinctly Christlike existence while avoiding defining its own beliefs "against" the world or other churches. Excellent!

Both are formed in relation to outsiders, but still each congregation is largely disconnected or independent from other congregations and parachurch ministries. And neither of these contemporary ways of organizing the church intentionally mirrors the divine nature of the triune God. So the structures set congregants free and focus them on others, but the arrangement itself is not a means of glorifying God. The distributed church is an attempt to use even the organization's structure to reflect the triune God we worship.

As we unfold the explanation of the distributed church, I will use references to both Scripture and Creation to describe the nature of God.

To paraphrase some of Francis Bacon's writing in *Advancement in Learning*, "God wrote two books." Christian scientists and theologians agree. He wrote one in the details of Creation; He wrote another one known as the Bible. The first "book" is called by theologians "general revelation." It is the way God reveals Himself, His being through the natural world (Romans 1:20). Theologians call the second book, the Bible, "special revelation." Revelation means exactly what it sounds like: revealing, or better yet, unveiling.

Because the distributed church seeks to be salt and light in the world, I will use references to structure that come from several different fields of study. I use these references not merely because they illustrate a way to arrange the church, but because the Bible says that our observation of the world is important for our understanding of God's action and nature.

In 1 Chronicles 12:32, the sons of Issachar are praised as being "men who understood the times, with knowledge of what Israel should do." On the other hand, Jesus rebukes so-called religious people who can read nature to see what the weather will be, but can't see God's patterns in nature. He asks, "Do you know how to discern the appearance of the sky, but cannot discern the signs of the times?" (Matthew 16:3).

We need to understand that we cannot only observe nature to see God, but that God will use nature in our (and its) redemption. Both the earth sciences and the social sciences can teach us much about how to form the church according to His nature and His current activities.

The Era of Connection

The era of postmodernism—the assumption that because everyone is confined to his or her own limited perception of reality, no one can claim to know absolute truth—is ending. That era hosted the predictable skepticism of universal formulas and the enthronement of individual interpretation and opinion. In other words, it was a philosophy alerting us to our limitations.

Being limited by our own cultural perspective is the result of history's boundaries, the Enlightenment's categories, the West's individualism and everyone's fear of outsiders (xenophobia). But as I shared with you in the prologue, we cannot be stuck inside our own perspectives for long without going insane. We cannot be satisfied defining life by what we can't know.

Christians are particularly fitted to go beyond the era of postmodernism. We are reconciled to our limitations, but not satisfied within them. That is why we believe that truth must be revealed to us. We admit our self-centeredness; that is how we know we need God's revealed perspective. Madeline D'Engle has quipped, "You have a point of view. I have a point of view. God *has* view."

Christians' problem with postmodernism is not the admittance that we only know partially: *Now I know in part* ... (1 Corinthians 13:12). We know we have only part of a larger truth; we just believe there is a larger truth. The postmodernists, who are resigned to living only in their own perspective, accuse Christians of being arrogant in claiming to know objective truth. But we do recognize another realm—a positive, substantive, more inclusive one. Life is not confined to one locality. Life is interrelated. It is an ecosystem beyond our imagination. *He is before all things, and in Him all things hold together* (Colossians 1:17).

But in this age, confined to our own perspective, we have come to believe that our thoughts are not only right, but complete. We have come to believe that our lack of relationships is not only right, but that we are complete without them. We have come to believe that our church is not only right, but complete within itself. We need a broader vision. We need the other parts.

Now comes the era of connection. Connection is not union. Connection is better. Connection keeps differences and appreciates their value. Connection does not shrink distances but uses distance to counterbalance parochialism. Connection seeks complementary partnerships and long-term support. Connection makes for peace not just by the minimizing of conflict, but also by the example of what it means to be whole. Connection realizes the purpose of our relationships with others, even those who disagree with us.

Connection is the way to completion. What we gain from others will increase what we have. What we give to others will elevate who we are. What we do with others will increase our impact. But how we connect with others will complete us.

We see this principle of connection within distributed systems throughout Creation, because it is the basic arrangement of God, of His divine nature (Romans 1:20). The examples are literally all around us. In addition to the micro and macro arrangements discussed previously we can see distributed systems within these venues as well:

- **Technology:** the Internet is the distributed model, with sites initially being able to connect with each other through a hub, so that they may one day be directly connected to each other, and beyond.
- **Sports:** Teams are distributed systems. Each sport is unique but every team's members are interdependent with each other as well as interdependent with the opponent in order to improve.
- **Business:** Franchises are distributed systems. Various forms of franchises have in common the strength of being both singular yet plural at the same time.

The arts, politics, international relations, universities—you name it, the distributed model at work in each realm.

A Vision of the Future

The chart below outlines the transition from the Industrial Era to the Information Era, ultimately leading to the Connection Era.

	Industrial Era	Information Era	Connection Era
Focus	Measurable Goals	Broad Issues	Influence by Relationships
Leader	CEO/Boss	Team Facilitator	Connector to outside resources
Worker	"Cog"	Resource	Co-worker/ Encourager
Worldview	Linear/ Production	Holistic/ Program	Catalytic/ Non-linear
Solutions Growth By	Reactive Accumulation	Proactive Expansion	Preventative Connection

Notice the progress from a mechanical approach to reality, through a conceptual one, to one of relationship. We will still use the elements we learned from the Industrial Age for a long time to come. And we will continue to benefit from the expansive knowledge and the holistic conceptualization of the Information Age. We have such a desire to know all about our subject of interest that search engines have become common verbs. Research is now summed up in a single phrase like, "Google it."

The emphasis is different now, however. We are beginning to understand that solutions and progress will come only from outside relationships and the perspectives they bring. We are not just individual inventors of solutions anymore; the unpredictable benefit of our service together is the most important part of the solution to any world problem. It doesn't just solve the problem; it prevents many new ones from arising because we have become interdependent.

The future of Northland, as just one of the churches that God will use to model this new connecting culture, turns on our realizing two meta-truths: 1) that God replicates His divine nature in Creation, and 2) that He expects His church to be a catalyst for that replication. Romans 1:20 states, "For since the creation of the world His invisible attributes, His eternal power and divine nature have been clearly seen, but understood through what has been made, so that they are without excuse."

What is this divine nature? Who is God, according to the Christian understanding of the Trinity? And why is the replication of that nature a secret to the effectiveness of the future church?

Before we answer those questions, we need to commit to a particular focus in rearranging the church ...

CONCEPTS IN CONTEXT
You, Christian, are a minister of the church.

Here are three challenges to help you personalize ideas found in Chapter Three.

- Think about the church for tomorrow: Review the mini-synopses in this chapter of these four different models of church today: "local church with a mission program"; the "emerging church"; the "missional church"; and the "distributed church." Decide which model of church you believe will help you most effectively minister and help to expand the Kingdom of God and get involved.

- Participate in the era of connection: Pray with another Christian that God would provide opportunities for you to encourage someone or some group that feels isolated and alone. Pray that you would be able to assist them in getting connected with others for worship and service.

- Consider your vision for the future: Think about what you have gained from others (your increase), what you have given to others (your privilege) and some ministry you have done with others (your impact). Consider ways you can use these experiences to connect with others for Kingdom purposes.

dis•trib´•ut•ed church (di-strib-yoo-tid chûrch)

noun

- A church that centers on God and revolves around others rather than insisting that "our church" is the center of the universe. This is a "Copernican Revolution" of the church.
- Intentional distribution of the church with a goal of ultimate connection through the kind of relationship that reflects God's image.

verb

- Putting the resources of the church as close to people as possible, offering meeting points and access to resources, in order to assist Christians in helping others.
- Connecting to outsiders and serving them where they are, rather than getting them to join us.

FOUR
A Church in God's Image

My father died when I was four years old. Cancer. For years my mother told me what a wonderful man he was. He was a war hero. He was fun and romantic. He was the love of her life.

I remember wishing that I could have known him so that I could be more like him. I could not get enough of an image in my mind to imitate him in any significant way. All the other boys I knew talked of their dads and picked up mannerisms from their dads. But I was on my own, or so I thought.

By the time I was in high school, I had one interest in life: football. My walk from our house to the football practice field took me past our town historian's house. Mrs. Hanno was a wonderfully interesting lady—for an old person who cared about dead people. Always able and willing to tell—interested or disinterested parties—who is related to whom, and how. She was the one with a memory for stories about people who had lived in my hometown.

She would sit on her front porch in the early evening, as most people did in those days. Often, when I walked by after football practice, she would shout to me, "Joey Hunter! You come up here, son. I want to tell you about your family." Of course I had to go sit with her on the porch, no matter how tired I was. Well-bred young people were taught to respect their elders.

Most days I would listen to her drone on about great aunts and third cousins twice removed. I had no idea what that meant. At that age I was not interested in extended family. But one day she started speaking to me about my father.

"Joey, do you miss your dad?" she asked.

"Yes, ma'am," I said, suddenly paying attention.

"I knew your dad. I knew his whole family. Good people. Your dad was a very responsible young man, Joey. I never heard anyone say a negative word about him. He loved your mother very much …"

By then I was hanging on her every word. Not many people would talk to me about Daddy Bill, as we used to call him. I guess they thought it would make me feel bad. But I was cherishing every word Mrs. Hanno was saying. Then she said something that would change my life.

"Joey, I want to tell you something. Every day I watch you go by here, and I am reminded of your dad. You have his mannerisms. You hold your body like he did. When you smile, it is his smile. When you are trying to be polite, even though you are really bored, you get the same expression he used to have. Joey, whenever I see you, I see your father."

I cannot describe what that did for me emotionally. For the first time I felt as though I belonged to my father, like I really had a father. For the first time I felt as though I was a part of him by extending some of his characteristics into the world. And for the first time I felt as though my life was not just my own, that I could live in honor of him. My life was a part of how he would continue to contribute to the world.

Each of us is fashioned after our heavenly Father, or as Scripture puts it, when speaking of Him in the plural, in "our image, in our likeness" (Genesis 1:26-27). We were not made to be orphans with some God-like qualities. We were made for continual connection to, and to be extensions of, Him. Because of Christ we don't just have the capacity to be unaware imitators; we know what His attributes are. We can intentionally reflect His nature in the details of our lives. That is not just a noble aim for each person. It is a noble aim for churches as well.

If, as Christians believe, the Truth is not a concept but a Person (John 14:6), then the organization of the church is not about structure but relationships—all of us being transformed into an image of that Person together (2 Corinthians 3:18).

The Distributed Equation

If we were to put the ontology (structure of being) of the triune God into a formula, it would look something like this:

I Am = Us for Them, There

I Am represents God's name or His divine nature, His being (Exodus 3:14). It can also represent the sense of identity of those who are made according to His image (Genesis 1:26-27). And it most certainly would represent a church that He is building to be His representative on earth (Colossians 1:15-20).

There are several aspects to God's triune nature (please note: I have spread these concepts over the next several chapters).

THE DISTRIBUTED DESIGN:
1) God is Both Singular and Plural at Once.

God is neither singular nor plural; He is both at once (I Am = Us). Scripture says that God is a "We" at the same time as being an "I." In the narrative of Creation, specifically Genesis 1:26, the name used for God is Elohim, a name that is plural in form, meaning "gods," yet it is used in the singular sense. Likewise, in the New

Testament, God is at once both singular and plural. The word "Trinity" is nowhere to be found in the Bible. An assumption of the Trinity, however, is pervasive throughout Scripture without being specifically defined (see Matthew 28:18-20; 2 Corinthians 1:21-22; Ephesians 2:18; 4:4-6).

Christianity is the only major religion in the world that understands God as Three-in-One. All of the major ecumenical creeds cite this understanding of God. The descriptions of the triune nature of God in the Apostle's Creed and the Nicene Creed are most clearly extended in the Athenasian Creed, which reads, in part: "We worship one God in Trinity, and Trinity in Unity; neither confounding the Persons: nor dividing the Substance. For there is one Person of the Father: another of the Son: and another of the Holy Ghost. But the Godhead of the Father, the Son, and the Holy Ghost, is all one: the Glory equal, the Majesty co-eternal."

His mysterious nature is reflected in the Creation, which is a combination of substances combined as one, yet still the parts can be identified as distinct in role and function. Jonathan Edwards, among other theologians, supposed that this character of Creation was a direct and intentionally designed image of the Creator. Edwards spoke of God's being as "disposition":

> "That is, God's essence is a constantly exercised inclination to repeat His already perfect actuality ... created being is relational ... a dynamic network of relationships, so that every entity is necessarily in relation to other—in fact all—entities ... 'A thing is only as it is related to other things.'"[2]

That reflection of God's being, that essential relatedness of different entities, is painted by Him on various canvasses of Creation. "For by Him all things were created: things in heaven and on earth, visible and invisible, whether thrones or powers or rulers or authorities; all things were created by Him and for Him. He is before all things, and in Him all things hold together" (Colossians 1:16-17).

God's being, essential relatedness of different entities, is reflected in the following:

- Physical ontology:

  Physicist Fritjof Capra wrote, "The great shock of the twentieth-century sciences has been that systems cannot be understood by analysis. The properties of parts are not intrinsic properties, but can only be understood within the context of the larger whole ... subatomic particles are not 'things' but interconnections among things, and so on. In quantum theory we never end up with any 'things'; we always deal with interconnections. That is how quantum physics shows that we cannot decompose the world into independently existing elementary units."[3]

- Biological combinations:

  Molecular biologist John Medina wrote, "Slime mold ... start their lives as free wheeling, single-celled, amoeba like creatures ... When the normal food supply is exhausted ... They join together and form a single crawling slimy organism ... termed ... a slug. Even though it is composed of many individual cells, this fungal Noah's ark moves as a coordinated unit, having both a front and back."[4]

- Anthropological development:

  Thomas Sowell wrote an article entitled, Culture and Equality, "Few, if any, of the great advances in human civilization have come from isolated peoples ... the size of a people's universe depends on how far they can reach out to other cultures. No great civilization has developed in isolation."[5]

- Early church development:

  When we read Paul's letters to the church communities in the New Testament, we see that each letter deals uniquely with a particular community, but they are not viewed as being separate churches. It was always "the church which is at … " (1 Corinthians 1:1) or "the churches of Galatia … " (Galatians 1:1), but they were viewed as parts of just "ONE body" (Ephesians 4:4). Groups of Christians meeting, no matter how distant or different from each other, were considered a part of one church.

The study of a wide range of various disciplines, such as physics, biology, psychology, sociology, business management and practical theology, reveals the singular-and-plural-at-once principle of structure. That principle reflects a singular-and-plural-at-once Principal.

Looking for Fellow Laborers

Both the distributed church and the missional church desire to do personal evangelism. In addition to that, the distributed church is always looking for partners with whom it can serve others in a practical way. Churches that focus on people only as potential recipients have an "us-them" mentality; the distributed church looks at everyone as a potential ministry partner.

A church focused on missions is life giving, but it contains a fatal flaw. Desiring to "lay down its life for others" as is Christ-like, has been interpreted in such a way that well-intentioned efforts inadvertently perpetuate an "us-them" mind-set. A separation, the dash, between "us-them" will eventually disconnect an ultimate joint mission. As long as one group sees another group as the object of its mission it will not see that group as a partner for serving others. If one group sees another group only as needy it is unlikely to see that group as a resource for furthering ministry. A distributed church thinks in terms of "Us." There is no "us-them" separation, just valuable distinctions. Jesus could not have paid for our sins as a substitution for us if He was not one of us or if we are not in Him. Understanding this plural aspect of God's nature transforms us.

When a young couple is falling in love, both individuals focus not just on each other, but they begin to picture a future together. One cannot think of doing something without estimating the effect on the other, or, even better, wondering how he/she can be included in the life of the other. Unity is the goal. And if they are Christian individuals, then that unity will express itself in serving God and neighbor. This is how the church should operate, not as corporation or school, but as Kingdom romance.

Evangelism is not merely explanation and persuasion toward Christian propositions; evangelism answers our mandate to build an extended family by helping others realize they, too, have been chosen by God the Father to serve along with us.

Group Matters

In the distributed church, small groups are not just personal places of connection; they are places of equipping for service in relationships that are outside the group. Because the concern of the distributed church is always for those who are not yet included, we structure the programs and actual physical buildings to connect us to others, not to protect us from them.

In the local-church-with-a-mission emphasis, the main focus is church programming. That is to say, the church accomplishes its goals through getting people inside a group, preferably within the church building. A distributed church promotes ad hoc groups to enable participants to be better spouses, parents, workers, community volunteers and neighbors. And the closer to their everyday activities that they meet, the better.

The local church has a tradition of making up its own plans, activities and principles to proceed into the future. The distributed church relies more on people who have identified a particular area of ministry ("area" being both biographic and geographic), then supports and equips these people in their calling. The local distributed church does not need to regulate all of the ministry that is proceeding from it.

One of the greatest compliments the leadership at Northland ever received was intended to be an insult. It didn't hit us that way:

Someone who attends Northland was behind two of our city's religious leaders in a buffet line at a city leaders meeting. The two were discussing the city's churches. Of course, they were not aware the person standing behind them attended Northland when one said to the other in a whisper, "Everywhere I go in this town, there is someone from Northland involved."

The other man said, "Yeah, I know what you mean. Those people are all over the place, but they can't control them!"

Exactly!

A local-church-with-a-mission program recruits people to do the jobs that need to get done. The distributed church does that too, to make sure the details of ministry on a week-to-week basis are taken care of, plus it offers the other 90 percent of the congregation (those who are not working "in-house": teaching Sunday School, singing in the choir, ushering, etc.) the encouragement and resources to address spiritual needs in their own spheres of influence. The distributed church commissions individuals in the congregation to use the gifts God has given them to serve their families, friends and communities.

The future of the local church with a mission program depends upon how many people can be recruited/selected to join the church in its efforts. The future of the church distributed unfolds as we can co-ordinate (co-ordain) Christians for their ministries, and offer ongoing encouragement to them where they live their lives.

Here are a few more comparisons of contrast:

LOCAL CHURCH WITH MISSION	DISTRIBUTED CHURCH
1. We / they	Us
2. Avoids or negotiates differences	Links with differences
3. Discipleship as reforming	Discipleship as partnering
4. Evangelism as crusade	Evangelism as finding family
5. Small groups as refuge	Small groups as training teams
6. Information improves position	Information improves outreach
7. Structure is to separate (holiness)	Structure is to connect (sanctification)
8. Focus is building, programs	Focus is "everywhere, every day"
9. Education makes bosses	Education makes servants
10. Accountability emphasized	Collegiality emphasized
11. Plan by principles	People are the plan
12. Boundaries protect	Boundaries connect
13. Clergy > laity	Laity = clergy
14. Worship as menu item	Worship as core: extended, applied
15. Complicated policies to obey	Simple directive: minister together
16. Join the church	Join other Christians to serve people in a way that brings them closer to God

The universal church is a compilation of Christians; all of us together are indispensable components in a magnificent body. As that body matures it becomes more coordinated. As we learn to co-operate we better represent the (Three-in-One) God we worship. But there are particular guidelines that come with that kind of partnering.

They are wrapped up in this second aspect of the triune God's nature ...

CONCEPTS IN CONTEXT
You, Christian, are a minister of the church.

Here are three challenges to help you personalize ideas found in Chapter Four.

1) Write down the distributed equation **I Am = Us for Them, There**: Think about the structure of God's triune being, summarized in this formula and consider how you should live in order for your life to reflect such a God.

2) Look for fellow laborers: Pray with another Christian that God will give you a heart for those who are lost *because* they are your "missing family members." Pray that you would have the courage and the opportunity to tell someone about Jesus this week. And when God gives you the opportunity to do that, make sure you also share with that person that a personal forever relationship with Christ gives him millions of brothers and sisters around the world. If the person you shared the Good News with accepts Jesus as his personal Savior and Lord, follow up as a spiritual brother or sister would and help him take his next steps of his faith journey and help him find a place to serve others.

- Group interactions matter: Check with your local church and see if they have a need for you to serve within the church walls. Every local church, including the distributed model, has several routine tasks that must be accomplished and important resources and classes that must be offered to equip Christians for service. The effectiveness of the church "out there" will be at its best when all is well on the home front.

dis•trib´•ut•ed church (di-strib-yoo-tid chûrch)

noun
- A church that centers on God and revolves around others rather than insisting that "our church" is the center of the universe. This is a "Copernican Revolution" of the church.
- Intentional distribution of the church with a goal of ultimate connection through the kind of relationship that reflects God's image.

verb
- Putting the resources of the church as close to people as possible, offering meeting points and access to resources, in order to assist Christians in helping others.
- Connecting to outsiders and serving them where they are, rather than getting them to join us.
- Arranging the church around the relationships of the congregation and partner ministries, rather than in and around a physical church building.

FIVE
A Church in Partnership

The natural world, from atoms to elements, from plants to insects to animals to people to groups, is in a constant search for the right partnerships. Right combinations make for stability, efficiency, sustainability and, ultimately, identity. This can be seen in a second aspect of God's nature.

THE DISTRIBUTED DESIGN:
2) God is a Perfect Union of Distinct Persons—Complementarity.

Each individual is made uniquely to need others; not just any others though, when it comes to cherished relationships. Unity with another person or group requires a particular fit. And we spend much of our lives trying to see what kinds of relationships to build with others. The Bible gives us a picture of that process in the story of the Garden of Eden.

In Genesis 2:8-3:24, we read that God is emphatic in His pronouncement against singularity: "It is not good for the man to be alone." Then, in a statement revealing His own nature, He continued, "I will make a helper suitable for him." God's perfect process involved a perfect match.

The words used for "helper suitable" mean "corresponding to or with." A part of that meaning implies that the two will be able to have ongoing conversations. In colloquial terms the translation is "one who answers back" or, in a riskier but more experientially true interpretation, "one who talks back." That's right, God made a partner for man who would "talk back."

In the intermediate time between that pronouncement by God and the bringing of the woman to Adam, God brings the animals to man to see what he will call them (Genesis 2:19-20). It is consistent with the word study to suppose that the man was not just naming them; he was calling out to them to see if they would answer back. Yet none of them is the right match for such an intimate relationship.

Here is the picture of God's nature and the secret to close relationships: The other must be enough like us to be intimate, but different enough to be necessary. That is the principle of complementarity for individuals and groups. We usually understand the "likeness" part of that equation, but often we overlook the value of difference.

Professor Henri Blocher writes:

"'Help' states plainly enough that the duality should not entail any rivalry. 'Companion' requires more, for the Hebrew term means literally 'as opposite him'; so the man and woman are not simply side-by-side—far from it! They must be genuinely different … the man must accept this otherness in order for the emptiness of his solitude to be filled."[6]

This principle of complementarity, being perfected by those enough like us to be intimate yet different enough to be necessary, is a reflection of God's nature of completion, and a guide to fulfilling and productive relationships.

Types of Complementary Relationships

There are two ways to live life. One is to take a stand and to combat anyone who does not agree with you. The other way is to take a stand (define your values and beliefs), then see how you can work with others who differ from you for the sake of making progress for everyone. As my friend Connie Rainwater puts it, "Find the common ground, for the common good."

Three kinds of complementary relationships can work to further our contributions to the world.

Complementary Relationship #1: Same mission, same methods. In these types of relationships we reinforce each other because we are communicating the same thing in slightly different ways and in different contexts. An example of this kind of relationship might be a best friend who agrees with you on practically everything but lives in a different context than you.

A church example would be much the same: many common characteristics, many common goals, but living in different places. In these types of relationships there is a camaraderie that is comforting and strengthening. Let me tell you about one such relationship between Northland Church and Kasr El Dobara Church in Cairo, Egypt.

Northland Church has a very close relationship with Kasr El Dobara. It is basically our same size, same theology, same staff composition, same heart and goal. We often joke that we are Kasr El Dobara in Orlando and they are Northland in Cairo. Yet our settings and challenges are certainly different, and we can learn from each other's culture, as well as exchange leadership.

The relationship began when one of our pastors met one of their pastors at a conference. A friendship blossomed, first between them and then between our congregations. Several of our pastors and lay leaders traveled to this church in Cairo to attend its leadership conferences both as teachers and as learners. Kasr El Dobara is much farther along in lay-leadership training than we are. We are learning much from them.

Kasr el Dobara has so many relationships globally that it is looking for better ways to stay connected, and so Northland Church has been able to help with some staff consultation, especially in the area of media development.

We have also experienced the joy of concurrent worship services with Kasr El Dobara. For one such occasion, in early 2001, we had scheduled such a worship service for the weekend of September 16. After the shocking 9/11 World Trade Center attack, we, of course, could not travel there. But since all the equipment was already in place, this Arab congregation came online to pray for us. We could see their congregation on the screen; they could see ours. Their pastors prayed for our nation and the Christian witness in the wake of the attack. We prayed for them also. Imagine how much it meant for our congregation to see Arab Christians praying for us just a few days after the attack! Both congregations were deeply moved by the overarching unity we found in Christ.

On another occasion, just a few months later, we had a full worship service together. I preached part of the sermon in English (translated into Arabic). The co-pastor from Cairo preached the other half of the sermon (translated into English). We each sang the same songs in our native tongues, with both languages printed on the screen. We taught them a uniquely American song; they taught us a uniquely Arab-Christian song. It was a full participation by both congregations, who could see each other and be personally greeted by the leaders who knew each other. We had tears of joy on both sides.

We are continuing to develop our relationship with Kasr el Dobara. In many ways, they have already perfected the distributed church ministry model. When they host an event, they never do it just for their resident congregation, they always invite outsiders. When they go to train others, they will do the training only if the host church has invited other churches that are dissimilar from the host church. We are learning much from their church, and are being completed by adding the Christ-like attributes of their culture.

Complementary Relationship #2: Same mission, different methods. We can also build relationships that are a significant extension or an expansion of who we are with people who complete what we do in a way that those who are similar to us do not. A church example would be churches of different sizes, locations, gifts or cultures that know God has put them together to complete each other. In these types of relationships, the differences help both parties mature.

Several years ago, I was in Ukraine with our partners there. There is a remarkable Association of Evangelical Mission Churches from whom we have learned much about how churches can cooperate together. I preached at a worship service where at least six congregations came together for that particular joint worship experience. Before the service began, the leaders of those six congregations came to me and said, "We want to take up an offering for a church in a country where the government may not look kindly upon Christianity. We were persecuted in the Soviet Union for many years; now we have a heart for other churches in hostile environments." I immediately thought of our partner church in Sri Lanka. That worship gathering in Ukraine took up a sacrificial offering and decided to pray regularly for that church in Sri Lanka.

A few years later, the distributed churches in Sri Lanka had a special project under way. In that Buddhist society, chanting is commonplace, but the Christian churches lacked music that could be used in worship services. Creating a uniquely Sri Lankan type of worship music became a goal of the churches. Northland staffers Zach and Laura Young flew over to help set up a recording studio. Months later, when a pastor from Sri Lanka attended a conference in Cairo with another one of our partners, he took some of the newly recorded worship CDs with him. And with the help of the church in Cairo, those CDs with the unique Sri Lankan sound are being copied and distributed to the venues where over one million Sri Lankans (many of them Christians) can listen to them in the Middle East! The prayers of the Ukrainian Christians to spread the Kingdom through the church in Sri Lanka were powerfully answered, not only in that island country, but in other parts of the world as well. Four partners all had a special part in extending the ministry together. None of us could have done that without the others.

Complementary Relationship #3: Different mission, different methods. The third category of relationships is complicated, and controversial to some. There are people God gives us to cooperate with who are very different in perspective and purpose. God uses those differences to clarify the positions of both parties. Relationships that hold together in spite of their differences have the potential of helping people within those relationships hone their beliefs and clarify their choices. Once that is accomplished the opportunity to serve others together becomes an option.

An example of such a relationship: ad hoc cooperation between or among a church, synagogue, mosque or government agency to accomplish an agreed upon project to improve the community. Such an ad hoc cooperation is not partnering in a spiritual sense. But because a distributed church isn't absorbing others into its likeness it can work with a variety of others toward a common good.

Some from Northland Church are developing relationships with the people in the Islamic Society of Central Florida. Imam Mohammed Musri and I are very different in our theology and culture, but we find in the time we spend together that our beliefs are further clarified and developed by those differences. We cannot be spiritually close, but we can be leaders who work together to better our community and create peace. I will do this to reflect Christ; he will do it to obey Allah. He and I need not be hostile in our differences.

There is one caveat that is very important to state after we have noted these three categories of complementarity: There is no category in which Christians can cooperate, let alone link, with sin. Obviously, a church would not be able to have an even ad hoc relationship with a drug cartel or a prostitution ring or the mafia, even to accomplish a project together that would improve the community. But a church must beware, as well, of partnering with believers who are ignoring the voice of the Spirit and the witness of Scripture.

Choosing to ignore a Christian's ongoing, intentional lifestyle of sin to link with him or her in any way that allows them comfort in their sinning is not something the distributed church would do. The Scriptures are clear about distancing ourselves from those who belligerently continue in sin (1 Corinthians 5:13). Nonetheless, even those interactions when unavoidable can be beneficial in clarifying our need to seek the holiness of God. When I see the destruction that comes from immorality and rebellion against God, I am very motivated to live a holy life.

Now we come to the third aspect of God's nature, embodied in our Lord Jesus Christ ...

CONCEPTS IN CONTEXT
You, Christian, are a minister of the church.

Here are three challenges to help you personalize ideas found in Chapter Five.

1) Complementary relationships with the same mission and same methods are a joy: Since the best relationships we have are often the last to get our consideration, because we know he or she will understand, take a moment today to call or email someone with whom you have a close relationship—someone who has the same desire you do to see God's Kingdom grow. Tell him how much you appreciate him and the opportunities you have to serve others with him. This is important because those we are closest to also need our attention. I have discovered along the way in ministry to never underestimate anyone's insecurities.

2) Complementary relationships with the same mission and different methods may need more attention: Tell someone you are struggling with that you are not willing to continue fighting with her. Then take a stand (define your values and beliefs) and figure out how you can work with her, in spite of your differences, for the sake of making ministry progress that will bless others.

3) Complementary relationships with a different mission and different methods are best if project-focused to benefit all: Study and know what the Bible says and what orthodox Christianity believes and then you can talk intelligently and serve alongside people of other faiths to accomplish a goal.

dis•trib´•ut•ed church (di-strib-yoo-tid chûrch)

noun

- A church that centers on God and revolves around others rather than insisting that "our church" is the center of the universe. This is a "Copernican Revolution" of the church.
- Intentional distribution of the church with a goal of ultimate connection through the kind of relationship that reflects God's image.
- **A network of churches sharing resources with one another, linking differences and bridging distances for the benefit of all.**

verb

- Putting the resources of the church as close to people as possible, offering meeting points and access to resources, in order to assist Christians in helping others.
- Connecting to outsiders and serving them where they are, rather than getting them to join us.
- Arranging the church around the relationships of the congregation and partner ministries, rather than in and around a physical church building.

SIX
A Church That Is Near

A few years ago, I was teaching at another pastors conference in Ukraine. One of the pastors raised his hand to ask, "What is the distributed church?"

I looked at the floor near his feet and saw a half-empty bottle of Coke.

"Did you have to go to America for that Coke?" I asked.

"No."

"Did you go to the bottling plant here in Ukraine?"

"No."

"Then where did you get it?"

"There is a vending machine one block from here."

"They must have a distribution system here so it is easier for you to benefit from what they have to offer, right? That is one aspect of the church distributed."

The very essence of the Christian faith is based on the nature of God, which is literally to "go out" and be among people. The doctrine of the Incarnation comes from understanding various passages of Scripture about Christ, such as Philippians 2:6-8: "Who, although He existed in the form of God, did not regard equality with God a thing to be grasped, but emptied Himself, taking the form of a bond-servant, and being made in the likeness of men. Being found in appearance as a man."

The Scripture tells about Christ going out to be among the people. He did not stay in one place expecting people to come to Him. Instead, He admonished His disciples, "Let us go somewhere else to the towns nearby, so that I may preach there also; for that is what I came for" (Mark 1:38). Love drives us outward.

The general principle to understand here, and one that comes directly from the Incarnation, is that God did not dilute His nature by His going out, but revealed it more fully. God did not become more distant from who He is by the Incarnation; He became more evidently who He is. He did not alienate part of Himself by coming closer to us; He demonstrated His nature, which is love.

THE DISTRIBUTED DESIGN:
3) God is Love and Goes Out for the Benefit of His Creation.

As the church becomes more involved in the world, it will also become more like Christ. Our risk "out there" will keep us closer to Him and cause us to be more like Him. Man is made in the image of God but as we go out to become His servants in this world, we are conformed to the image of Christ (Romans 8:29). This is true for individuals and also for churches

What are the "going out" activities of the church? We have thought of going out only in terms of missionary activity, but is that the only paradigm that will bring the Kingdom into the world? When Jesus was on the earth, did He not give us numerous examples of loving our neighbor? His self-chosen job description involved serving the poor, captive, sick and oppressed (Luke 4:17-21). His church has the same job description. Why would the church not partner with other components of society—government, business, the arts and education—that can be of assistance to those in need? The church needs to fear less what it could lose and dare to consider what everyone has to gain through "for such a time as this" partnerships. Who knows, representatives from the categories of society we choose to assist might become interested in our Motivation.

The church will only find its complete identity in going out to serve both the physical and spiritual needs of the world. When Jesus taught us to pray, "Thy kingdom come, Thy will be done on earth as it is in heaven" (Matthew 6:10), He was dedicating us to a vision of earthly life that can best be accomplished if the church "has left the building."

How can we love our neighbor completely without being involved in the improvement of the society in which they live? Christians must be involved in the shaping of public policy and that means, among other things, we can't ignore politics. When Jesus said, "Render to Caesar the things that are Caesar's; and to God the things that are God's" (Matthew 22:21), He was not just talking about paying taxes. Citizens owe the systems under which they live as they have benefited from them.

In a democratic society the government expects our participation. We need to voice and vote our values. Some Christians need to serve in government office. We each need to "go out" and be a witness by living an exemplary life, serving, and giving our input.

Christians need to serve in every part of the culture in which we live. Businesses need individuals who will work as unto the Lord (Colossians 3:23), both in attitude and work ethic. The arts need Christians who will see and express Creation in a way that glorifies God, translating His beauty and depth. Education needs dynamic, loving, Christian men and women who will teach accurately God's sciences and humanities in a way that produces wonder and appreciation in the generations to come.

In all of these fields and myriad others, we Christians need to see ourselves as "sent" by God into the world of everyday life. That is the church distributed.

Ultimately, when you keep going out to the people whom you serve, you want to be near them on a permanent basis. That's the way it was with Jesus when He transitioned from a physical servant to the Holy Spirit. And that's the way it is with His church when it transitions from a building-centered local church to a field-based church.

This leads us to the fourth aspect of our God's nature, which emphasizes His nearness as the complement to His transcendent majesty …

THE DISTRIBUTED DESIGN:

4) God is Near to Us as the Complement to His Transcendent Majesty.

From the beginning, the Spirit of God was hovering close to the world's disorder and emptiness (Genesis 1:2). It is from that closeness that God speaks to the darkness of the world and begins the creation of new life. In the Spirit, God is not only transcendent and other than Creation, He is also near and involved.

It is not surprising that Christ's ongoing presence and redemption for the world is carried on by the ever-present Spirit (Matthew 28:19-20; John 14:16-17). It is the nature and strategy of God that divine help is near to those who need Him. God does not demand that man make the journey to Him. He knows that we cannot. Instead, He has made the journey to us; He is near to us wherever we are. He is our comforter, counselor and guide.

In like fashion, the church needs to be near to people, offering meeting points and access to resources, in order to assist Christians in helping others. We have a saying in our culture, "I'll be there for you." Wouldn't it be great if that were a geographic reality instead of simply a reassurance of availability? Instead of requiring people to travel to be a part of the church community, parts of the church community and resources need to be positioned where people live.

The church should be as good at helping the individual Christian or even another church do its ministry as any business is at helping customers. I think of the American office and print services company Kinkos, providing office and print services 24/7: Customers may or may not need personal assistance, but a staff person stands ready to do whatever aspect of a project the customer requires to accomplish the goal. An effectively distributed business model like Kinkos should be a wake-up call to the church. Here's a business that has figured out how to offer resources and personal support for office needs near where people actually live and work. How much more important is it for the church to be able to offer its resources and personal support near where people actually live and work for the purposes of ministry? Structuring church like this gives those who desire to serve others the assistance they need to be productive and helpful.

You may wonder how this structuring of church differs from "a church on every corner" that many urban/suburban landscapes offer. It differs in that the distributed church is identified by its interaction with people of a community more than its building location within that community. It is more about helping people personally turn the corner to a better, more fulfilling life than it is about getting them into the building on the corner for a program. Interacting directly with the world, and increasingly present in it, the energy of the church can significantly impact a wide range of people in a variety of circumstances and environments.

We are the body of Christ (1 Corinthians 12:27). We are His place of physical habitation on the earth. His Spirit in us is a way He influences the world.

By distributing parts of the church (people groups and individuals) away from the main structure (the church building), the church can be more "on site" in the lives of its people and the lives of the people it desires to bless.

In the development of the early church, this distribution is exactly what we read about in the book of Acts. First, there was the establishment of a church in Antioch that still related to the mother church in Jerusalem (Acts 11:19-30). Then there was a proliferation of churches nearer the people. The principle of "being near to be with" is demonstrated through God the Father to Jesus, His Son; from Jesus to the Holy Spirit; from the Holy Spirit to His people, the church; and now from His body, the church, to the world.

"On site" support for those who affect the world everywhere, every day is a valuable aspect of the distributed church.

The Clustering Effect

The fifth and final aspect of God's nature that we will explore is another variation of God's singular-and-plural-at-once being, only it has more to do with group gathering than with unity that comes from personal relationships ...

THE DISTRIBUTED DESIGN:
5) God Is Relational and Seeks to Connect Isolated Christians With the Groups That Will Increase Their Capabilities.

The principle of clustering is first introduced in the Creation story. God congregates those living elements of like nature so that they can have the closeness they need in order to thrive. We learn in Genesis that He "gathered" (Genesis 1:10) "after their kind" (Genesis 1:11, 12, 21, 24, 25). God has valued groups from the beginning.

The summary of God's character, togetherness, is described in His Word and seen in His Creation. It is also seen as He creates a people on a journey together (Genesis 12:3) so that the rest of the families of the earth can be blessed. It is also evident as Jesus gathers the disciples to follow Him and be of mutual support in ministry together. And, finally, it is part of the function of the Holy Spirit to unify us for the benefit of others (Philippians 2:1-4).

Written into the DNA of Creation is a group instinct. Beginning with individual needs, a close examination of most of nature will cause us to conclude that individual survival and effectiveness is dependent upon group living. Despite having some discomforts (competition, need for cooperation, contamination, etc.), group living is advantageous for survival. Groups of species thrive by interacting with each other and with species different from their own. And in doing so they reflect God, who is relational.

Gilbert Waldbauer, in his book *Millions of Monarchs, Bunches of Beetles*, writes:

> "Being a part of a group—be it a cohesive unit or only a loose assemblage—can benefit an individual in several ways: A group may be better able to cope with adverse weather than can a lone individual. Group defenses against predators or parasites may be more effective ... Groups may be more efficient at finding food and subduing it if it fights back ... Finally, associating with many others of the same species usually simplifies the problem of finding a mate."[7]

Clusters (multiple groups) cooperating with other clusters, even beyond a particular species, is well-known to those who study how the world develops. The mutual benefit of this inter-group arrangement predates, but extends to, human development. Evan Eisenberg, in his book *The Ecology of Eden*, writes:

"Alliances of species were remaking the world long before

we came along ... 'Mutualism'—a relationship between two species that yields greater population growth for both—is a slippery term ... most will involve some predation or competition. Yet the whole tangle taken together does seem to form a commonwealth of interest ... it can also be called by a less slippery name: symbiosis, which simply means that two species live in close and near-constant contiguity ... symbiosis has allowed the partners to colonize or conquer new environments." [8]

This "group DNA" of God is best seen in His crowning achievement—people (see Psalm 8). Humans have always been studied in their natural groups. More recently, students of business and sociology have coined the term "social capital." Don Cohen and Lawrence Prusak, in their book *In Good Company, How Social Capital Makes Organizations Work*, explain:

"Social capital consists of the stock of active connections among people: the trust, mutual understanding, and shared values and behaviors that bind the members of human networks and communities and make cooperative action possible."[9]

Social capital makes an organization, or any cooperative group, more than a collection of individuals intent on achieving their own private purposes. Many real advantages accrue to the organization as a whole.

Cohen and Prusak go on to explain the relevance of social capital to our specific time in history:

"We are long past the time when any one individual can know virtually everything worth knowing ... or everything he needs to know to do his own work well. So belonging to the networks ... has become essential ... their capacity to form connections with one another ... is now more important than IQ, the measure of individual intelligence."[10]

From the beginning, God has created most of nature to thrive in groups. He also called groups of people to form even closer and more purposeful groups (Genesis 12:1-3). Jesus called not one or two disciples, but a group of them (Matthew 10:1-5). Clustered around the throne in heaven there are people from every group (Revelation 7:9).

God expands our capabilities by relationships within groups and also through relationships between and among groups. The distributed church seeks to connect isolated Christians with the groups that will increase those Christians' capabilities and benefit the groups as well.

The principle that we are made complete by outside differences isn't limited to the person-to-person realm; there is a valuable realm of ministry congregation-to-congregation. The church matures by maintaining various degrees of closeness, with several other churches and parachurch ministries. Clusters, whether in the form of networks or affinity-based cooperatives, make the church more complete. Groups within a cluster need to be enough alike to be intimate (in varying degrees) but different enough to be necessary. Such is the nature of complementary relationships.

Partnerships: The Future of the Church?

The future of the church is veiled. We can see it partially, though, by the partnerships that are now forming throughout Christianity. God is connecting us. Ministries are working more closely together than ever before. A great example is Team Resource.

Team Resource of Central Florida held its first meeting on 9/11 in 2001, not because of the tragedy in New York City, but because that just happened to be the day that some caring people decided it was time to come together to form an action plan to help the needy. The first Team Resource meeting brought five groups together: a church (Northland), a homeless shelter (Anthony House), a job placement agency (Christian Help), a clothing and financial relief organization (Christian Sharing), and a legal consultant (Paul West and Associates) for the purpose of pooling resources to help "the least of these."

After several years, more than 170 churches, ministries, nonprofit organizations and local government agencies have participated in the monthly Team Resource meetings to break bread (pizza, wings and chocolate actually), fellowship, and share stories of how God is working in and through each of them and the people He puts in their paths. Meetings bring together African-Americans, Caucasians, Hispanics, Asians, Democrats, Republicans, Independents, Pentecostals, Catholics, Presbyterians, Methodists ... well, you get the picture. This is the community of believers at its finest. They don't spend this time criticizing the federal government or playing party politics or pushing religious agendas. They meet as a family to share resources and to praise the God from whom all blessings flow.

In 2006, Northland began to partner in an even broader community, through the development of an Internet network: ConnectCity. Resource Point, a project of ConnectCity, is a network of local multi-denominational and ethnically diverse churches. Interconnected for the purpose of serving people in need, participating churches register resources (individuals, programs and services) with the network. Let me give you an example of how this works. Let's say a man comes to a local Community Church that is a part of the Resource Point network and he is looking for a car because he can't work if he can't get to his job. A church staff person can check the Resource Point website for the listing of resources available from any of its participating churches.

If the Baptist Church has posted that it has a car to donate, the Community Church staff person can turn back to the man and say, "We have your car." In other words, every church that is part of the network is able to better meet the needs of those who come to them for help. It's personal. When churches work together like this, it expands the resources of each participating church. Resource point also coordinates Christian response during times of disaster.

That all sounds good, doesn't it? Churches throughout America can develop such effective connections for service. It will take tenacity since the church has had centuries of training in effective disconnection ...

CONCEPTS IN CONTEXT
You, Christian, are a minister of the church.

Here are three challenges to help you personalize ideas found in Chapter Six.

1) God is near, and so we as His church should be near: When you become aware of a practical need someone has, pray for her and help her out as best you can. Maybe that involves you personally doing something for her, but it might mean you need to assist her in finding out where and how her need can be met. Remember, do what you can, with what you've got, where you are.

2) Clustering: Groups connecting with groups promotes huge ministry progress. Get educated about denominations and parachurch ministries that have chosen to combine their resources and efforts to work together for Kingdom purposes. Global Networks (www.call2all.org) exists to connect Christians within the different spheres of society: church, government, business, science and technology, arts and

entertainment, in service of fulfilling the Great Commission. The National Association of Evangelicals (www.nae.net) is a 30-million member organization that effectively gives a voice to American Christians. The World Evangelical Alliance (www.worldevangelicalalliance.com) does the same on a global scale. Visit their websites and others to find out how you can be part of a Cluster ministry.

3) Partnerships that invite the world to a brighter, more godly future are critical: Bring your gifts and the specific passion you have been given into partnership with a group that specializes in a focused aspect of Christian service. Your ministry outreach and the group's will be expanded. You can find Christian groups that serve God with expertise in a specific field by Googling "Christian (your interest area)." A few varied specialty groups that you might want to explore: justice issues—International Justice Mission (www.ijm.org); marriage and family issues—National Coalition for the Protection of Children and Families (www.nationalcoalition.org); Creation care issues—Creation Care (www.creationicare.net).

dis•trib´•ut•ed church (di-strib-yoo-tid chûrch)

noun

- A church that centers on God and revolves around others rather than insisting that "our church" is the center of the universe. This is a "Copernican Revolution" of the church.
- Intentional distribution of the church with a goal of ultimate connection through the kind of relationship that reflects God's image.
- A network of churches sharing resources with one another, linking differences and bridging distances for the benefit of all.

verb

- Putting the resources of the church as close to people as possible, offering meeting points and access to resources, in order to assist Christians in helping others.
- Connecting to outsiders and serving them where they are, rather than getting them to join us.
- Arranging the church around the relationships of the congregation and partner ministries, rather than in and around a physical church building.
- Connecting with neighboring Christians for support and encouragement and to better serve their communities.

SEVEN
A Church for the Times

A History of Walls

The Emperor Constantine's conversion gave the early fourth-century church more favor than it could handle. Over the centuries that followed, the church became preoccupied with its own self-importance and preeminence. Instead of seeking better ways to love and serve, it fostered an "us-them" mentality, which, unfortunately, carried over into the Reformation.

Since the foundation of the church, the term "church" has been understood in terms of divisions of the church. Many think of a local congregation as "the church." Some think of their own denomination as the real "church."

This is not a condemnation of local churches or denominations. Many such churches and denominations arose as a needed theological and/or organizational correction to the existing church. Reasons for disconnection and increasing separation varied; they were not limited to "I would rather do it my own way." There have been, since the beginning of the church, individuals who personalized the faith and joined with like-minded others as an expression of the church that reached yet another section of the population with the message and compassion of Christ.

Jesus' concern was for the kingdom of God. When He said,

"I will build my church" (Matthew 16:18), He was not stacking up bishops in His head. Kenneth Scott Latourette said:

> "To him the Kingdom of God was both a present fact and a future consummation … It was not a state with physical boundaries, but embraced by men [and women] who continued to mingle in ordinary society … it is one of the strange and momentous facts of history that out of a movement begun by one who paid so little attention to organization and administration has come … elaborate ecclesiastical structures."[11]

Very early in the church's development the apostles made a simple division of labor (Acts 6:1-6). Some of the leaders would devote themselves to prayer and the teaching of the Word, while others would see to the administration of help. As the church grew, it continued the Jewish custom of appointing elders to oversee the congregation of believers (Acts 20:17, 28; 1 Timothy 3:1-7). Yet within these very simple organizational lines, the chief characteristics were unity and outreach. The church in Jerusalem held a preeminent place among the churches, but not a centralizing place. "Preeminent" means first and very important, but "centralizing" implies control. The first indicates influence; the second indicates restriction. The church did not set out to isolate itself.

In fact, the first-century church planter, Paul, was preoccupied with connecting the churches because his Holy-Spirit-given theological conviction was that there was but one church in many places (Ephesians 4:4-6). Much of his concern was to help the church mature with the reminder and practice of unity, even at its earliest stages. Latourette said:

> "He shared the conception of a Church which embraced all Christians, sought to promote the unity of that Church and to heal its divisions, and to bind in sympathy the communities which he had founded to the mother one at Jerusalem."[12]

In the first three centuries, as Christianity spread among the different geographical sections of the Roman Empire and beyond, each congregation had its own "personality." We can infer such dissimilarities from the different problems addressed in the letters Paul wrote. The problems in Galatia were not the problems in Corinth. The pattern of regional differences continued throughout the growth of the church. Yet there was a sense that there was only one church, and that it would include differences, both within congregations and between congregations, and not be divided by them. The church was even intentionally inclusive of those differences. Latourette wrote:

> "In the first three centuries … while it was still frowned upon by the state, Christianity had spread to most and possibly all the main divisions of the Roman domains … over-passed the boundaries of Judaism, and … Hellenism … It had won important footholds among the non-Greek peoples of Egypt and the Latin-speaking peoples of the West … Although bearing the marks of its different environments, Christianity was already more inclusive than any one cultural tradition."[13]

The other mark of the early church was the pattern of growth that resulted from its immersion in ordinary daily life. The early church was not armed with evangelism tools and strategies, as we are. Christians did not stop their conversations about the faith as they exited the church. In those conversations the ancient Christians included the "regular world," the people they worked with and lived beside. Latourette, in *The First Five Centuries*, wrote:

> "The chief agents in the expansion of Christianity appear not to have been those who made it a profession or a major part of their occupation, but men and women who earned their livelihood in some purely secular manner and spoke of their faith to those whom they met in this natural fashion."[14]

All of these factors advanced Christianity's amazing growth and successful overall unity. In addition, from the very beginning the church built networks of Christians to respond to the crises around them. From epidemics to persecution, the Christians would survive and serve because of their relationships with each other. Not only were the Christians noticeably different because of their theology of eternal life, but also because they took care of one another—and even took care of those who were not Christians. What a contrast to the pagans around them who just tried to save themselves or their own! The broader practice of love and care translated into better chances of survival for the Christians and a very attractive witness to others. Rodney Stark, Baylor University Professor of the Social Sciences, said:

> "Christian values of love and charity had, from the beginning, been translated into norms of social service and community solidarity. When disasters struck, the Christians were better able to cope, and this resulted in substantially higher rates of survival … Alien to paganism was the notion that because God loves humanity, Christians cannot please God unless they love one another. Moreover, such responsibilities were to be extended beyond the bonds of family and tribe."[15]

What Happened to Divide Us?

What happened? How did we come to be divided? It was probably success and the self-serving vanity that followed. When the Emperor Constantine became a Christian and made Christianity the preferred religion of the realm, the community of Christians did not need each other in the same ways. They could now afford disunity without perishing because of it. Their differences were no longer put into perspective by a hostile culture. Local churches at different locations had existed in the same spot for long enough that each became native to that culture. That is not bad, of course; it just had a distancing effect among churches. The church was a catholic ("catholic" simply means universal) church, but it was beginning to show signs of division. Latourette says:

> "Theoretically it knew not racial, cultural, or geographic divisions. Actually, however, it was inclined to take on the colour (sic) of the various regions and peoples among whom it was found and to divide in accordance with them. No organization or appeal to an ideal, a person, or a doctrine proved strong enough entirely to thwart the drift and often outright schism followed. Christianity took on many different forms … Monasticism came into being and, while remaining within the church, divided it into two main groups of Christians—those who thought of themselves as seeking to conform perfectly to the commands of Jesus and those whom they regarded as having in part compromised with the world. Division amounting eventually to actual schism took place for reasons that combined geography, race, and culture, with, usually the added bitterness of theological views."[16]

Those factors also apply to the Reformation and beyond. Two major developments influenced the church in the 1,000 years intervening between the time of Constantine and the Reformation.

First, the parish system developed. The parish system has been the central paradigm of the church for at least 1,200 years. The understanding of that system, which was at its zenith during the feudal/manorial era of economics, is this: a local church is at the center of a geographical area (parish). The local church is the center of the life of that area (since it is supposed that all the people should be Christian). All the people of the area are responsible to be loyal to that church. Since this idea was devised in a Christian era, in Christian lands and endowed by powerful Christian leaders, and since no one did much traveling, it made sense. Later in history, when different local churches inhabited a territory, the assumption was slightly modified to, "Be loyal to one of the churches near you."

Second, the spread of Christianity by the various expressions of the monastic movement had a profound effect beyond official church doctrine. A more active and passionate variety of Christianity acted as a missionary movement within and without the church. The Cluny movement, for example, sought to purge the Roman Catholic Church of chronic abuses of nepotism, sexual immorality, and financial greed. Later, but with the same passion, the Jesuits sought to spread the Gospel in many lands, with much sacrifice. In all of these movements, this monasticism:

> "… remained within the fold of the official church and did not question the creeds. Yet in practice it introduced novel emphases and altered popular religion … bringing a fresh enthusiasm for Jesus."[17]

It is important to note that revival was taking place inside and outside the official church long before the Reformation. It did so because of the close relationships of some church members with the people beyond church walls. To make these missionary enterprises successful, support from the people was essential. Since the missionary movements were a non-necessity to the survival of the traditional church, the power for them had to come from grassroots personal initiative. To win the support needed for mission work, the leaders had to make a more direct appeal with biblical truth and spiritual vigor.

The Reformation (when the Protestants split from the Roman Catholic Church) moved the church toward popular participation. In the Protestant version of Christianity, the emphasis is on each person being in relationship with God through studying the Bible instead of having a relationship with God mediated only by the church. Indeed, the concept of the "priesthood of all believers" eventually made the Bible, rather than the territorial church, the center of reference. Protestant Christianity is better characterized as being "by the people" rather than "for the people."

To be sure, as Protestantism developed, the parish system (or territorial churches) stayed firmly in place. Williston Walker, in *A History of the Christian Church* states:

"In Saxony, which became the norm in a general way for the creation of territorial churches ... the land was divided into districts, each under a 'superintendent' with spiritual, but not administrative, superiority over the parish minister ... A Lutheran state church ... was substituted for the old bishop-ruled church. Other territories of Evangelical Germany were similarly organized."[18]

On a broader scale, though, a more radical type of geographic division was taking place. Each national environment began to foster its own forms of Protestantism. Because there was no overall figure of unity (Pope), and no one governing body (Cardinals), the separations of the Protestant churches were much deeper than those in the Roman Catholic Churches. Latourette wrote:

"In many respects Protestantism was as much political as religious ... In several lands where it prevailed it did so because monarchs or princes saw in it a means of enhancing their authority. National feeling, the aspirations of special classes, and the cultural characteristics of particular regions all entered into the shaping of Protestantism."[19]

The elements of division within this new form of Christianity grew. The differences of theology and personality were translated into divisions of the church. In many cases, acrimony was so unleashed that the "other" was assumed to be lost to the Kingdom. Latourette wrote:

> "Zwingli and Luther were in many respects in substantial agreement, but they were temperamentally unlike, and their religious experiences had been very different. Luther declared Zwingli and his supporters to be no Christians, while Zwingli affirmed that Luther was worse than the Roman champion, Eck ... The Roman party rejoiced at this evident division of the Evangelical forces."[20]

The tragic comedy of these developments, in retrospect, is that even though the Protestants claimed to be more at liberty to interpret Scripture for themselves, they assumed that only the voices inside their own denominations could be correct. They were trapped within themselves, and, again, as I stated in the prologue, that is a definition of insanity. Unfortunately for a few of the most devoted disciples of the Reformation, such is still the case. It is almost axiomatic in Christianity today that the most conservative (or fundamentalist) churches, devoted to the concept of the priesthood of all believers, are least likely to associate with any believers but their own.

The question must be asked, in light of the heritage of the geographically limited organization and the "only those who think like me" perspective of theology, whether the church can ever reflect the universal presence of its universal God. Scant evidence exists that the church, as it has been traditionally arranged, can be distributed "into all the world," reflecting our overarching unity in Christ. In fact, the preponderance of evidence suggests the contrary.

So a majority of local church workers have learned to operate life virtually alone. That is also true for the majority of Christians.

Me, Myself and I

It is not just the church that has suffered from the predisposition toward independence. Self focus rather than partnering characterizes many issues facing our culture.

Human cloning is not only a major issue, but also a major metaphor of our time. The debate is now moving beyond whether humanity begins at conception, implantation, viability or after birth. The debate is now about whether the source of ingredients to form a baby should come from one or two people. It is not only an important issue ethically; it is a telltale issue culturally. The ethics cannot be reduced to issues of physiology, or of determining when a soul enters a person. The ethics now must answer whether or not true life is defined by needing others. Is another's input (literally) at the core of who we are? Is it crucial to the fulfillment of our potential?

Reproducing ourselves, without the input of "outsiders," has just recently come to biology, but the church has long had its own versions of cloning. When an individual "disciples" a new believer into only his own Christian worldview, he can all too easily reproduce only himself. When a large church plants a daughter congregation in order to create a little version of itself, and chooses not to cooperate with other ministries in the birth, that is a form of cloning. When a parachurch ministry focuses on reproducing only one specialty field but does not influence its constituents to partner with other parts of the church to complete their unique calling, it is reproducing itself.

The local church congregation is, more often than not, sufficient unto itself. What does a local congregation feel that it needs from the outside? With the possible exception of wishing it could be the recipient of a large donation of money, or an influx of people that would become assimilated into it; the traditional local church congregation doesn't sense the necessity of relationships with other ministries. Some who occupy its pews see even its involvement in mission efforts as a distraction.

It is not good …

CONCEPTS IN CONTEXT
You, Christian, are a minister of the church.

Here are three challenges to help you personalize ideas found in Chapter Seven.

1) Each of us has a history of walls: Ask God to knock down the ones that are blocking you from a life of connection for ministry.

2) Divisions are not the problem, attitudes about them are: Talk to someone you have been avoiding. Respect differences and connect with others. Both are things Abraham Lincoln did well. His motto: "I don't like that man. I must get to know him better."

3) The divisions that exist between Christians today are just part of the problem: Unlike the early church, we tend to divide our lives between the "church world" and the "regular world." How can you integrate your faith more into your everyday life?

dis•trib´•ut•ed church (di-strib-yoo-tid chûrch)
noun

- A church that centers on God and revolves around others rather than insisting that "our church" is the center of the universe. This is a "Copernican Revolution" of the church.
- Intentional distribution of the church with a goal of ultimate connection through the kind of relationship that reflects God's image.
- A network of churches sharing resources with one another, linking differences and bridging distances for the benefit of all.
- **A way for the church at large to benefit from our differences, being perfected by those enough like us to be intimate yet different enough to be necessary.**

verb

- Putting the resources of the church as close to people as possible, offering meeting points and access to resources, in order to assist Christians in helping others.
- Connecting to outsiders and serving them where they are, rather than getting them to join us.
- Arranging the church around the relationships of the congregation and partner ministries, rather than in and around a physical church building.
- Connecting with neighboring Christians for support and encouragement and to better serve their communities.

EIGHT
A Church Turned Right Side Up

Young in the pastoral ministry, wanting to do a great job for God, I was eager to learn about all the people in the congregation at Faith United Methodist in Princeton, Indiana, including the ones who never came to a church service. One day, I noticed a dad with his three boys attending a worship service. Assuming the mother had died, or the couple was divorced, I inquired of another parishioner about what had happened to the family. "Oh, the mom is still in the family," he assured me. "She just never comes to church." Thinking I could welcome her to church, I decided to call on her.

That afternoon I knocked on their door several times (I could hear the television on inside), a well-dressed woman opened the door curtain, then the door itself. "Hello. I'm Reverend Hunter, the new pastor at your church, and I came to meet you. I've enjoyed getting to know your husband and boys … " I never got another word out.

"Come in, Reverend!" I was startled by her friendliness. Here was a woman obviously not angry with the church, as I had expected. In fact, as she continued to talk, I assumed just the opposite. I assumed that she very much wanted a relationship with church and with me.

She continued talking very rapidly, telling me all about herself, what she believed, her philosophy of being a wife and mother, what she knew of the town, and advice on how to be a good pastor to the congregation. As she continued to talk non-stop I kept looking for a place to chime in. But there were no pauses in her stream of words. I was beginning to wonder how she was breathing. I could not detect any sign of her inhaling. My conclusion was that she was a woman who wanted relationships and intimacy so much, that she was frantic to have a conversation with me.

After almost two hours, I still had not said a full sentence. I was late for another appointment, so I got up to leave. She did not stop talking; she just got up with me. I started backing toward the door. She still did not stop talking. Finally I was outside and she shouted, "Goodbye. I've enjoyed our conversation!"

Later that day, I was talking with an older minister who was mentoring me. "Today, I think I met the loneliest person I've ever seen," I said, "She was so desperate for companionship!"

"Really?" he said, "What gave you that idea?"

"She never stopped talking," I said. "It didn't seem like she was even stopping to take a breath! How is that for wanting intimacy?"

He smiled one of those "bless your heart; you don't get it" smiles.

"Don't you understand, Hunter? She wasn't seeking intimacy; she was avoiding it. As long as she kept talking, she was in control. She didn't have to respond to any agenda or questions of yours. She talked incessantly for the same reason she hasn't been to church: She was avoiding outside relationships."

Oh.

The church is largely an institution that talks about itself incessantly. It communicates what it is doing. It advertises its programs and its teachings about how to live life. It opens the doors to anyone who will listen, but that does not mean that a local church is a place open to outside relationships. Staying in our own house (institutional church building) is a way that some Christians choose to keep away from others.

The world needs churches that are finding their way out of institutionalism. Institutions have precise definitions and policies and consistent methods to which one can adhere. Institutions are conceptually oriented, neatly defined and clearly developed. Institutions tend to require obedience over spontaneity and rote memorization over creativity.

The church is called to be an assembly of relationships or, at least, of those people who want to be in relationship. It is not supposed to be primarily an institution that conforms people to its programs. If we are like the Christ we worship, we are not on earth to be served, but to serve (Mark 10:45). Although that may sound like a cliché, it is the most difficult of feats to accomplish, because the institution tends to prevent real outside relationships.

We must begin to see all of life as ministry! In the distributed church model, husbands and wives see their roles in the marriage as ministry. Moms and dads see parenting as ministry. Employers and employees see work as ministry. Students are in ministry in their schools. The church is simply the people who are growing in relationship with God and with others. Together for the breaking of bread, fellowship and prayer (Acts 2:42), people who are part of the distributed church family, worship God along the way. Whether gathered together or serving apart, ministry happens everywhere, every day, when the distributed church model is practiced.

Worship, Serve, Equip

Northland is based upon three simple acts that can help people to serve more effectively: worshiping, serving and equipping. Everything begins and ends in worship.

Relationships are the point, but worship must be the context.

Worship is what we will be doing in heaven. Worship is the re-orienting activity on earth. It fine-tunes our orientation toward God and our hearts toward one another.

Worship

Worship gives us the proper perspective. We do badly with human relationships because we think the issues are all important. They are not. But how can we remember that without worshiping the Christ who did not need to win battles in the flesh to win the larger victory of the heart?

Worship gives us the opportunity to partake of the nature of God—in Word (teaching from the Bible) and sacrament (elements commuting the Spirit of God). Worship also lets us partake of God's nature in the fellowship of the believers. In the congregation is the body of Christ. Each part of His body is unique and distinct, and has a purpose that ultimately completes our own. Worship gives us a glimpse of our eternal wholeness with others as the bride of Christ.

Worship reminds us of the grace of God, and relieves much of the pressure we feel to manage everyday problems perfectly. God's grace and sovereignty ensure our success in His plan.

Worship focuses us on the reason for our existence: to reflect and glorify God. "We all, with unveiled face beholding as in a mirror the glory of the Lord, are being transformed into the same image from glory to glory, just as from the Lord, the Spirit" (2 Corinthians 3:18). The focus on God, not our own efforts, is the foundation for our transformation.

Therefore, everything we do and all that we are should begin and end in worship. The way Northland frames church looks like this:

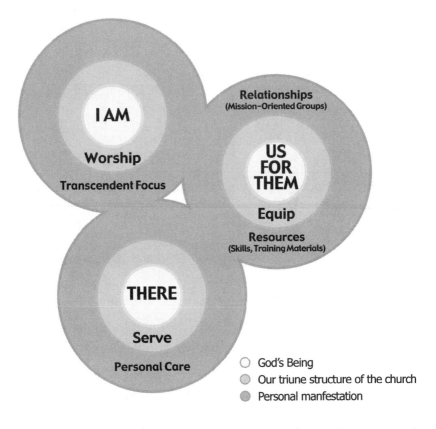

Worship in a Northland service is a combination of historic and contemporary elements. In the worship music, readings, visual arts and sermon we intentionally include elements that will affect people emotionally, provoke them to search deeply and challenge them to reason. We then encourage them to apply that worship development in their daily lives to the benefit of their "neighbors," regardless of the geographical distance of those neighbors. In other words, we reinforce the Great Commandment every week: "Love the Lord your God with all your heart, and with all your soul, and with all your mind ... You shall love your neighbor as yourself" (Matthew 22:37, 39).

As a Christian serves others, he is reminded of the training and support he needs to become a better servant. A church can shape its "equipping" portion (training and supportive relationships) to be most helpful to those who already "labor in the field."

There are ways of equipping people for ministry (service in everyday life). The question that needs to guide our plans to equip them is, "What do Christians really need from the organized church to serve the individuals and groups in their everyday lives?"

A few general areas of resourcing Northland has discovered:

- **People need to be inspired by and taught the Scriptures in corporate worship services.** Our worship team develops a worship experience around a particular text of Scripture every weekend, but it is simply a venue for the Holy Spirit to communicate personally and directly to people. Unless people acknowledge that God is inspiring them to serve others, any effort they make will be short-lived and work (not worship) oriented.

- **People need examples of relationships that complete and elevate each other's abilities.** Vernon Rainwater (the pastor who is our worship leader), Tim Tracey (our executive director of worship), and I (the preacher), very obviously need and enjoy each other in our part of the work. As a leadership team we are a weekly example of interdependence.

- **People need practical instructions.** Of course the sermon always has some application points, and we have in our handed-out weekly bulletin (it's actually a 20-page newspaper that is also posted on the church website) information about personal ministry and equipping opportunities. Northland has three main areas when it comes to equipping:

  — ESSENTIALS—Every Christian needs to be taught the basics of accurate theology, personal devotional practices and how to share Christ as they serve others.

  — TRAINING—Every Christian requires specialized

training that corresponds to what they are actually doing in life. Topical Bible studies on marriage, parenting, finances, business as ministry and conflict resolution, among others, are consistently made available.

— RELATIONSHIPS—Every Christian needs supportive relationships to fulfill their lives and to be sustained in ministry. These may be found in an affinity group (men's Bible study) or a short-term topic-based group (such as a *Purpose Driven Life* study group) or simply in the supportive atmosphere of a few friends who get together to encourage and pray for each other as they prepare to serve others in a way that will bring them closer to Christ.

- **People need church recognition of life transitions.** Clergy call these "sacerdotal functions." People need to be baptized, married and commissioned. They need their children dedicated, and a funeral when a loved one dies. A representative of the church, in some recognized form, is important and effective in marking such transitions with ceremony and reverence. And of course the taking of communion (another sacerdotal function) is central to our worship and is the physical symbol of our receiving the nature of God.

- **People need some sort of ongoing support "in the field."** They need someone from the church who is accessible to them. This philosophy pervades our relationships with both local and distant partners. Through resources and relationships we get to be part of how people serve others in their area of the world.

Empowering the Congregation

We commission the people who worship with us to initiate ministry. We welcome their efforts and will do whatever we can to help them in their ministry. Most of our resources and relationships come from volunteers, not from professional staff.

So we want to equip each person according to his or her giftedness to serve others (1 Corinthians 12:7). We address biblical content, basics of our faith, personal devotional life-patterns, and help in living the Christian life, but much of what we need in order to serve others well must be tailored to our particular gifts and calling. Churches must develop large-group worship, small (inter) group connections, and personal team support because God speaks to us in the midst of multitudes, in the midst of unique groupings, and in the personal voice of someone who knows us. In these settings, people are able to discover their strengths and their passions for God's purposes.

When the church equips congregation members through relationships and not standardized systems only, it is much more likely to see spiritual maturity result.

Righteousness in Relationships

Becky and I have always enjoyed working together, even in our beginning days of ministry. When I needed to visit congregation members in the hospital, she would bundle up all three boys and go with me. They would wait in the lobby area while I made my rounds, then we would go to our next destination. We often ended our daily travels in the parking lot of the local grocery store where I would stay with the boys while she ran in for a few items.

I remember vividly a day when I was wondering about our oldest son's maturity. Specifically, I was wondering if he was noticing girls yet. I didn't have long to wonder.

An adorable little red-haired girl came out of the store. She had curls that bounced and a dress that floated on petticoats. Her shiny shoes accentuated her lacy socks. Even the package she carried was dainty and cute.

As she climbed on her bicycle, which was as gleaming and fancy as she was, I noticed our oldest son Josh's eyes. They were fastened on her. He stared steadily at her while she rode past our car until she disappeared around the corner. He seemed absolutely enthralled.

Finally, he spoke up, "Wow, Dad, did you see that?"

"See what?" I teased.

With a tone of longing, he answered, "That bike!"

I knew he still had some growing up to do. An unmistakable mark of maturity is a fascination with people rather than with mechanized systems or vehicles of progress.

Remember the Pharisees, scholarly men, preoccupied with doing right things according to the system? Their focus was not people; it was mechanics of the system. There is a mark of righteousness, though, that exceeds the righteousness of the Pharisees. It takes into account the well-being of a relationship.

Years ago, I did a study on the word "righteousness." I was deeply touched by the writings of Elizabeth and Paul Achtemier in the *Interpreter's Dictionary of the Bible*. A summary sentence for their study of that concept throughout the Bible could be stated: Righteousness is meeting the demands of a relationship, whether with God or with man.

There are, of course, objective ethical standards: the Ten Commandments are a primary example. Yet "righteousness" has to do with how to rightly behave in a particular relationship. Righteousness (meeting the demands of a relationship) is as relevant in partnerships among ministries as it is in communicating the Gospel to those unfamiliar with it. It is especially necessary in partnering with ministries very different from our own.

Any Institutional Church Can Become Distributed

Many people are skeptical or even critical of the institutional church. Disappointed by the difference between the impact it should have and the impact it actually has had on the world, some have walked away from church altogether. Criticism motivated, though, by a desire to improve the church is a good thing.

The distributed church is neither a counterbalance to nor a polar opposite of the institutional church. It does make the assumption, however, that neither an individual nor a congregation can develop to full maturity on its own or within a closed system. The distributed church is defined by the quality of *outside* relationships being developed by its people, and by the congregation as a whole. The distributed church uses organizational strength to go beyond institutional boundaries.

Open-Source Ministry

A closed-source system is one of two schools of software program development in the computer world. It is a system with specific parameters, and any user who wants to purchase it and work within those parameters will find it capable. In the computer world, closed system software has made a few people, such as Bill Gates, very rich. It has also made millions of people, like me, very passive. In the church world, the same thing happens. Anytime we consign ourselves to one particular set of Christian materials or methods—only Charismatic, only Reformed, only Catholic, etc.—we are not only limiting ourselves to one piece of Christendom, we are not engaging in the learning conversations that could benefit ministry. The more materials we can survey and the more Christians we can learn from the more we will be enabled to come up with the most effective ministry we can offer our context. An unwillingness to glean from another Christian's biblical understanding is "insider" vs. "outsider" mentality and promotes disconnection.

An open-source system, in which all can contribute, is healthy. It invites creativity and the continual improvement that comes from sharing. In the computer world, this open-source revolution is an opportunity to contribute for the good of all. This is not a world of "us" vs. "them." This is not a world of resources being guarded for the sake of profit. Open-source systems invite more people, perspectives and components that anticipate the unexpected and ultimately produce greater results. Wikipedia, a multilingual, Web-based, free content encyclopedia project written collaboratively by volunteers from all around the world is an example of an open-source system. Anyone familiar with it understands why it will be those who connect others to outside resources, and especially those who can help interpret it, who will be the leaders in this era of connection.

In nonprofit organizations, especially in the church, the goal is not profit but changed lives. Lives are changed when people get involved personally in order to make a difference. Church distributed encourages Christians to devise local solutions that suit them better than a generic program could. At the same time, a church distributed encourages Christians to share what works in their specific situation with others. The more specific solutions there are available to the larger body of Christ, the greater the possibility that a shared solution may be one that fits perfectly in additional situations. Leaders need to engage in "best practices" discussions with other leaders so that the church as a whole can expand and mature from multiple points of leadership. That kind of participation not only fills people with a sense of purpose but best reflects the God who engages us as co-creators ...

CONCEPTS IN CONTEXT
You, Christian, are a minister of the church.

Here are three challenges to help you personalize ideas found in Chapter Eight.

1) Worship God: Regular worship with others is critical to your spiritual walk. Don't miss "entering His courts with praise." It is critical for your relationship with God and for your ministry service to have impact for Kingdom purposes.

2) Practice righteousness: Do what it takes to fulfill the demands of the relationships in your life. To honor God, be the spouse, the parent, the friend, the neighbor, the employer or employee, the citizen that you need to be for those with whom you have a relationship.

3) Seek some ministry partners who have open-source systems: They have much to bring into the relationship. Listen to the perspectives of others and encourage their input. Encourage someone you know to take the lead in a ministry God has placed on his heart.

dis•trib´•ut•ed church (di-strib-yoo-tid chûrch)
noun

- A church that centers on God and revolves around others rather than insisting that "our church" is the center of the universe. This is a "Copernican Revolution" of the church.
- Intentional distribution of the church with a goal of ultimate connection through the kind of relationship that reflects God's image.
- A network of churches sharing resources with one another, linking differences and bridging distances for the benefit of all.
- A way for the church at large to benefit from our differences, being perfected by those enough like us to be intimate yet different enough to be necessary.
- **A comprehensive model in which spiritual maturity will continue to develop through generations of relationships.**

verb

- Putting the resources of the church as close to people as possible, offering meeting points and access to resources, in order to assist Christians in helping others.
- Connecting to outsiders and serving them where they are, rather than getting them to join us.
- Arranging the church around the relationships of the congregation and partner ministries, rather than in and around a physical church building.
- Connecting with neighboring Christians for support and encouragement and to better serve their communities.

NINE
A Church That Motivates Leaders

When the first team of astronauts arrived on the moon, the world was watching the incredible event on television. As Neil Armstrong descended the ladder from the spacecraft to the surface of the moon, he paused just before he stepped onto it. That last step was more than a meter in length. As he jumped onto the surface of the moon, he said, in a well-thought-out phrase, "That's one small step for man, one giant leap for mankind."

Some steps are bigger than others, both in distance and in the preparation it takes to get there. Yet each step is just a step.

The step from being a local church to a distributed church is not a simple one. The mental distance one has to traverse to get there requires great focus in the midst of doubt. It is the job of leadership to see the possibilities of outside partnerships, and to train the congregation in that way of thinking. The benefits of going outside for inside maturity will be questioned by many in a congregation, just as those who said, "We spent that kind of money and went through that kind of effort for a few moon rocks?" But the effect of that step on the way a congregation thinks of itself both corporately and individually is "giant."

A step can be as practical as scheduling time outside our everyday routines. The leap can be as significant as becoming a world leader.

But neither will happen without acting upon an innate desire, planted in us by the relational (triune) God. We were made in His image; we are prompted to go out as He did. Through intentional steps that take us beyond our own "world" and into the worlds of others who need us, we, as well, will be completed.

We live in a complex world and leadership in a complex world is different from leadership in a simple one. In a simple world, leaders direct people. In a more complex one, leaders direct less and inspire more so that people will be challenged to trust in God for their personal, biblical understanding of what to do.

Leadership, in the long-past modern world, was a simple, direct-control relationship, no matter how many tiers of organizational structure it went through. Accountability was the key word. Chain of command was the clarification. Leadership in the connected (relationship) world is motivation toward what is ready to be birthed. In the traditional sense, this definition of leadership may sound too vague. But in the biblical sense, the leader is just the one who challenges people to "get moving," and our inspiring God is the One who directs the steps (Proverbs 3:5-6).

The idea of the Messiah being a servant rather than a commander of armies was so troublesome for many that they misunderstood Him. His statements that He could do nothing without the Father have puzzled Christians who narrowly interpret leadership as directing one group instead of providing a way for everyone who wants to do the works of God.

A mature leader in normal circumstances distributes control. That is to say that a mature leader recognizes the limitations of confining an organization's development only to what he or she can oversee. A spiritual leader, though, recognizes that he or she never really had control in the first place. The sovereignty of God is working itself out no matter what the decisions; it is just that the decisions can make the trip better or worse.

A leader fills two crucial roles in a group. First, he or she is the convener of the group. Every group needs a central component that will embody their togetherness. A leader offers that. He or she may be a poor visionary or an even worse organizer, but the need of the group to have both a structural and symbolic head (as in ancient Israel's desire for a king) will eventually emerge. The origin of that image, of course, is that we all were made to follow the King of kings and the Lord of lords.

The second role of a leader is that of being ahead of the rest of the group in walking toward the future. That may seem like a rather tepid definition of leadership, but a leader is not a god who makes the future happen; he or she glimpses more of the future before others see it, and heads there.

One day our son Josh came home from elementary school and announced that he had been the leader of the class that day. My pride immediately leapt to the conclusion that he had exhibited some natural charismatic gift that revealed his superiority in some way. I asked, "How did you get to be the leader?" He answered, "Well, I learned we were going to the library together, so I just walked faster than anyone else."

Much of leadership is no more glorious than that. We as leaders discern where we are being directed (Spirit led) as a group, and we, at least in awareness, get there ahead of others. We are not superior in intelligence or specialized ability, but somehow we have learned where the group is headed. How do we learn that? We can read both the signs of the times and the ability of the group. We know what the group does well and what it doesn't. And we know the general leadings of God as taught in Scripture. A mature leader can recognize the supernatural gifting of a group, just as he or she can see it in a person. Groups have gift mixes and personalities just as people do. Groups also have a residing potential as individuals do. Ways that leaders discover that potential include familiarity with:

- Successes the group has experienced
- "Watershed" turning points in the life of the group, to understand how God has used them to benefit others
- Painful experiences of the group's past
- Strengths of the group in connection with the context (denomination, city, upcoming opportunities, etc.) to which it relates
- What the group could add to other parts of the body, and what it needs from other parts of the body to complete its potential

In the end, the vision must always be positive. We are here to add to or fulfill the positive. All of God's attributes are positive; all of Satan's attributes are negative. That tells us something about both our goals and our attitudes.

Leadership in the era of connection is not limited to reading the signs of the times, seeing the potential of the people, and pronouncing the group's fullest expression. Leaders add something personal and unique. Leaders can make a great difference to the group and to history by contributing themselves, a personal ingredient that could not have come from anyone else.

Leadership is not management. Leadership is a relationship that gives confidence to those who want to make a constructive difference. Confident people build their own relationships once they are launched from a group. Impactful leaders enable and empower groups to build relationships with one another; they encourage clusters. There is no more important component for achievement than a Christ-centered empowering relationship. In nonprofit organizations, relationships that lead to changed lives are triumphs. But even in profit-making organizations, good relationships are necessary for success.

In our Christian faith, the main component of our relationships is Christ, not religious knowledge or moral perfection. The goal is not winning, but loving and serving. Loving service trumps the fulfillment of individual accomplishment and the distributed church prizes that kind of service. Ironically, loving service also accelerates accomplishment.

The reason that demonstrated love facilitates accomplishment is that it increases interchange. The learning, the adjustment, and the improvements that come from that interchange are keys to progress. God doesn't limit His people to each individual's progress; He called a group to be His people.

Preparing a Distributed Church

The future is uncertain to everyone but God. Times of significant and rapid change call for a different type of planning than was possible in the past. When I was a young minister, the churches that were paying attention to the future had a "Long Range Planning Committee." The assumptions of these types of committees were that the:

- Congregation will be basically the same group for years to come.
- Building (these committees usually focused on facilities) would be the central place for answering the congregation's needs.
- Congregation itself could be managed to stay fairly stable in makeup and worldview by setting church goals.
- Church would have the same role in society that it had maintained for decades.

The dynamics of planning for the future are different today than they were in the "modern age" of the industrial society. Then, the future could be neatly added onto the past. Facilities could add a wing or a family life center or even a new location because the church simply built upon what it had been in the past. Church programs could be designed to meet the presumed needs. Most church programming was on site and came out of discussions about problem solving rather than ones about realizing potential. Most planning for future staff could be done by first designing job descriptions for the predictable programming and then going after the most qualified person to fill that position.

Now, and in the days to come, even the church, as slowly as she changes, is waking up to some surprises. The small church cannot count on existing in the future. The middle-sized church cannot count on having a full-time minister, let alone having ministers to lead in expanding programming. And the large, growing church needs a much different type of programming and staff than it once did. It is not just providing a room, a good program and a leader that counts now. The challenge, rather, is to know whether the type of programming in the past—that counted on a relatively stable family unit and a fairly consistent attendance—is a foundation for the future.

The needs of people are different now. We have gone from simply needing a safe Sunday school room to needing a system for spotting non-custodial parents. We have gone from having a good lesson out of the Bible to first explaining what the Bible is and who God is. We have gone from the women's guild meeting in the church parlor to "12-step" groups meeting someplace where they can step outside for a cigarette. We have gone from a few in mission committee meetings directing funds to many going on mission trips … from getting the liturgical colors right to including people of all colors …

from arranging potluck dinners to feeding the poor. Ironically, there is at the same time a deepened and renewed interest in the more liturgical and mystical side of Christianity, especially among many of the younger generation. In any event, one style does not fit all, or even the same person for very long.

How can we plan for a future that we cannot predict? Actually, part of the future is predictable.

First, we predict the future when we accurately acknowledge those things that will never change, such as our need for relationships. We were created in the image of God who is, as the creeds tell us, a relationship (Father, Son and Holy Spirit) and who is love (1 John 4:8). Therefore, whatever we build for the future that focuses on the improvement of relationships will be relevant.

Second, we can predict the future when we see those things that will inevitably change. The speed of communications, the accessibility of knowledge, the globalization of the world, and the resulting juxtaposition of differences, are not up for a vote. They are happening now and will continue happening at a rapid pace. Therefore, whatever we do to help people continually adjust to differences will be relevant.

Third, we can predict part of the future by actively determining what we are going to add to the general church. The future is not crafted merely by examining concepts and cosmic forces. God designed people to add their unique ministries to the whole church. The book of Acts, which tells of the building of the church, is, in large part, the biographies of very peculiar personalities, not merely a theology spread geographically. We can tell what part of the future will be like when we build our part.

Planning for an Unknown Future

We can plan for the years to come only to the extent that we come up with steps that could provide for any of the possible futures. There is a type of planning that is called "scenario planning." A good reference book on this type of exercise is Peter Schwartz's *The Art of the Long View*. The genius of scenario planning is its flexibility. Even though the future may resemble one of several different scenarios, the preparation for the future can be suited to fit any of those possible scenarios.

For example, at one time Northland Church had a building plan drawn that included a traditional sanctuary. That project would have cost $26 million, and few of us were highly motivated to invest those kinds of funds on that building. We questioned whether it would be the kind of structure that would be most useful for the future. If we exploded in growth, would it be expandable without millions more being spent? If fewer attended, could we justify such an expense? If we decided to move, who could buy such a building?

One option that we discussed was building a temporary facility. Built to last ten years, it would cost a fraction of the price, would let us expand the congregation, and then if we decided to build the expensive sanctuary we would have a larger church community to support it. A temporary facility would not be a financial burden or embarrassment if the congregation dwindled. It would also be moveable if God called us elsewhere. It was a next step that would prepare us better for any of our likely futures.

As discussions of options continued, it became apparent that the best option for us, would be to build a virtual "communications center" with capabilities that could potentially connect us with an unlimited amount of other sites for worship, teaching and non-local conferencing. We did build a new sanctuary, but it does not just seat a few thousand, it virtually seats an unlimited number of worshipers via interactive connection with any number of worship sites. Its sanctuary and classrooms can be linked to anywhere in the world.

Scenario planning can be achieved in areas of programming and staffing as well. Planning that does not need to know the future, that has "along the way" flexibility, is best. Programs that can be adjusted or be deleted and some staff that is contractual—rather than hiring only permanent part-time or full-time employees—is also helpful. The most significant challenge is to build long-lasting relationships in the midst of changeable structures.

Even with permanent staff, ongoing job adjustments for the best possible future together ultimately result in stronger relationships within the team. Permanence of staff relationships and overall mission are prized more than permanence of organizational structure. Staid and rigid organization drains enthusiasm. Change, even the anticipation of change, for the sake of a purpose greater than an organizational chart, builds confidence in the purpose and importance of working together.

While a leader is powerless to determine the details of the future, and therefore must make plans that will be of use in any scenario, a leader does have an advantage when it comes to visioning the future. A leader sets the culture, or general atmosphere, that will establish what kinds of people and possibilities find an environment in which to thrive. Will people look forward to the challenges and changes coming? The leader is the one who will communicate optimism or dread about the future. He or she does help people move ahead with a picture of what will be, but it is the leader's personal encouragement to others toward the adventure of finding out what will be that most affects the future.

Build the Right Environment

The greatest organizational principle of leadership is laid down for us in the first chapter of the Bible, Genesis 1. Before God made any particular life form, He made the environment that would allow it to thrive. Before He made the birds of the air (verses 20-21), He made the expanse of the heavens (verse 8). Before He made the fish and the great sea monsters (verses 20-22), He made the seas (verse 10). Before He made the beasts of the earth and people (verses 24-27), He made the dry land sprout with vegetation (verses 10-12).

The first organizational principle for leaders is this: Every group needs an appropriate environment that will allow it to thrive. Without that special environment, the group will break down. The art of building such a specific environment is part of leadership.

The basics needed to build a healthy local church are the basics needed to build a healthy distributed church. The consistency and security of a local church is a God-designed setting for the growth of Christian relationships. These essential ingredients of a Christian's development are best established within a local church:

- **Worship corporately.** Since our purpose in this life and the next is to glorify God, and since our main source of spiritual growth is to be fed by Him in His Word (the Bible) and to experience His sacraments (especially communion), worship together is essential.
- **Fellowship with Christians.** From the earliest of times, the continual meetings of different sizes of groups (large—"politea," middle—"oikonomos," and small—"kiononia")

have been the environments needed to nurture Christians.

- **Train disciples.** From the very earliest of times, the local church gathering has provided some form of teaching or training after an individual makes a commitment to Christ. The earliest known document to help young or new believers grow in their relationship to Him was called the "Didache." Such training, and, additionally, Christian leadership training, remain essential for a healthy church.

- **Reach out via mission efforts.** Sharing our faith and blessings with others is fundamental to our beliefs. This is the very essence of the Christ we worship, the One who was sent out, and we cannot be complete without being sent to others.

In addition to these four essentials in the local church, the nurture of a distributed church requires these additional ones:

- **Serve to foster reciprocal relationships and closeness to God, not just to export yourself.** The missionary movement had both good and bad effects. It spread the truth of the Gospel; it also spread the impression that others need us more than we need them. Essential to a distributed church is the understanding that our maturity has to do with learning as well as loving and helping. "The eye cannot say to the hand, 'I don't need you!' And the head cannot say to the feet, 'I don't need you!'" (1 Corinthians 12:21, NIV).

- **Teach from a worldwide/interdisciplinary perspective.** In addition to the foundational truths and practices of Scripture, the sovereignty of God over the whole earth should be demonstrated by a spectrum of teaching that notices "the real world." This latter phrase is used by secularists and Christian cynics to note the "spiritual only" myopia of the church. The integration of other branches of learning will demonstrate "all truth as God's truth." "For by Him all things were created: things in heaven and on earth, visible and invisible, whether thrones or powers or rulers or authorities; all things were created by Him and for Him. He is before all things, and in Him all things hold together" (Colossians 1:16-17, NIV).

- **Build relationships outside the congregation as part of life together.** Just as our truth has been disconnected from the "outside world," so has our fellowship. Most churches do not see relationships to other ministries or to non-Christian neighbors as essential to their spiritual growth. But they are. "He said to them: "You are well aware that it is against our law for a Jew to associate with a Gentile or visit him. But God has shown me that I should not call any man impure or unclean" (Acts 10:28, NIV).

- **Connect with other Christian groups in worship.** The act of worship noted in Revelation 7:9 is both international and intercultural worship. That cannot be effectively achieved in a local congregation, even with representatives from different groups present (though it's a good start). The act of connected worship can and should happen periodically. This is important not only to reflect the biblical glimpse of the circumstances in heaven but also in celebration of our relationship with other groups of believers.

Build the Right Governance

I pray this prayer: "Lord, let me help your people, not in proportion to how much I know, or even how much I pray, but in proportion to how much they need." Governance is not mainly a function of planning or executing policy; it is mainly a function of serving according to a need. In principle, the only difference between governing the masses and helping a neighbor is the number of people involved. Yet civil government, like church government, is most helpful when prompting citizens, not government agencies, to solve humanity's challenges.

A governing structure oriented from and toward the kingdom of God is about meeting the demands of a relationship. Whatever form government takes (there is no exclusive right form of governance in Scripture), the task of governing is always the same: Give people what they need and stay in a close relationship with them. Whether the government is for a country, or a business, church, classroom or family, the principle remains the same: responsiveness to needs so that people can be most productive and helpful. Those who govern need a structure that will allow them to get an accurate assessment of the needs of people and they need a spirit that inspires people to service, not one that controls them. A few suggestions may help:

- **Know the difference between polls and provisions, and govern by the latter.** Governing is never fully democratic (someone has to make a decision), and leadership by acquiescing to the popular opinion is no leadership at all. Listening to people is good, but if a leader has to hear what to do from a group, it is already too late to lead. Provision, on the other hand, is exactly what it sounds like. It is the kind of forward (pro) looking (vision) that will anticipate what people will need in order to be productive. Since every culture, nation, church and family is different, the needs for each will be unique.

- **Create a structure that emphasizes what people do well, instead of one that fears when people do ill.** Governing has become almost synonymous with safeguarding (at its best) rather than encouraging. While the former is necessary for a sense of security, focusing on it is not. If a government intends on being of any use other than keeping order, it must be positive in its orientation. Focusing on the special abilities of people in a given nation, business or family increases the likelihood of productivity and fulfillment. Leaders focusing on fear to motivate will exhaust both people and resources that could be used for betterment. Leaders need to be positive!

- **Create a structure that will link with other organizations naturally (not just leader to leader).** As a puzzle maker plans at the outset that the pieces of a puzzle will make a great picture when placed correctly together, leaders who are able to design a structure that promotes both learning from and investing in others will be most effective. Such governance produces results that exceed an historical parochial focus. When the temptation to do only what is good for "your own group" disappears, the best outcome can be realized.

- **Create a structure that tries to put itself out of business.** The glory of a government is in its nonuse, not its use. The ultimate success of a government is the maturity of its people to the point of independence from government, and interdependence with each other.

- **Create policies only when you must.** Governments tend to make policies rather than deal with people. Making a policy is easier than facing painful conversations. But policy begets more policy, not better relationships. To keep it in check, don't make a policy without taking time for conversation with those who could be hurt by another policy.

Finding Common Ground

The Western culture has been limited by logic when it comes to choices. Our favorite pseudo-intellectual polarizations are a simplistic view of a moral God who casts everything in terms of right or wrong, and an opposite view, pluralism, the assumption of no absolute right or wrong, just allowances for the way different people believe. Each of these polar opposites has a corresponding method of governance.

The church that is based on "either/or" thinking will have a permission-based governance. It will tend toward an extreme form of accountability (phrased in a language of quality control or religious purity) that ultimately comes to its apex and bottleneck in a leader or governing board. The assumption of this type of leadership is that there is one best way to conduct life and church, and it is up to the leader to follow it, and to get other people to follow it. Either one chooses the right way, or one chooses the wrong way, but one cannot have it both ways. Compromise becomes synonymous with surrender. The colloquial phrasing of this perspective is summed up in the phrase, "There are very few, if any, gray areas. Everything is either black or white."

The church that is based on "both/and" perspective will have a minimalist, passive governance. The leadership will be "tossed here and there by waves, and carried about by every wind of doctrine" (Ephesians 4:14). Quality concerns, in an environment of allowances for individual theology and morality, have more to do with protection of free expression than either truth or love. If no one can declare truth for anyone but himself or herself, or at the most a particular ministry, then what rallying point is there, except perhaps the art of the expression itself?

Leadership That's Personal

Neither the "either/or" choice, nor the "both/and" pluralistic non-choice is adequate for church governance. Both of these ways of addressing differences display a lack of understanding others, and deny the fact that God has a purpose in differences.

The ultimate paradigm in thinking is "various ... so that ... " It does not preclude occasions where "either/or" choices are appropriate, or "both/and" is correct. But the "various ... so that ... " paradigm implies the constant need to respond most accurately to each person or opportunity. This paradigm goes back to the principle of complementarity and to the definition of righteousness. Our decisions must spring from the basic tenets of our faith and must be made in precise responsiveness to fit the person and occasion.

When my three sons were growing up, I decided to give Josh, the oldest one, a pocketknife. I wanted him to learn how to handle one, and in those days, owning one was a symbol of adult responsibility. My middle son, who had a delightful personality, but was so accident prone he could somehow manage to fall into his food from a sitting position, wanted a knife also. When I said, "You are not ready yet," Isaac cried, "That's not fair!"

As they grew up, it turned out that a knife would be most appropriate for my third son, Joel (a surgeon); a book for Isaac (a pastor who reads as voluminously as a scholar); and hunting and sports equipment for Josh (an organizational management guru who loves to hunt and compete in triathlons). But I digress ...

Isaac was right, of course. Life isn't fair. Leadership isn't a matter of being fair. Leadership means choosing to respond very personally to an individual's development and capabilities. The

God who chose Jacob over his older brother, Esau, to lead Israel does not respond to us simply on the basis of "both/and." Just as the Father distributes to each one what is good for the whole body (1 Corinthians 12:7), He also gives each of us the particular resources and relationships we need to exercise those ministry gifts (1 Samuel 19:1-3; Acts 5:33-42).

Our leadership must imitate the One who from the beginning (Genesis 1) set particular environments for varied and unique kinds of living beings.

Lead from Multiple Points

The distribution of Christian leadership as a way of management is better than directions from a single point person or particular level of leadership. Much of Christian leadership is simply helping people take their next steps toward Christ and ministry.

Northland could not function if any more than a fraction of the decisions had to come through any particular person or small group of us. Each Northland staff member knows more about the specific field of ministry in which they work and serve than any of the rest of us does. Each one has to be ultra-capable so the rest of us are released from having to take any significant responsibility in that part of the ministry.

In my younger days as a pastor, I was occasionally mentored by Carver McGriff, the senior pastor of one of the largest United Methodist churches in the country. One day I asked him this question, "Why do so many churches stay small when they are trying so hard to grow? The pastors I know are great people, they preach good sermons, the people in the congregation are talented, but the average size of the churches is pretty small. Why aren't they growing?"

His answer was immediate and accurate.

"Because," he said, "most pastors will not permit anything to happen in the church without personally knowing about it and, in most cases, approving it. Anytime you limit the activities of a church to what one person can understand, you are going to have a pretty small church."

I never forgot that insight. It has served as a warning to my own tendency to want to control everything at Northland.

Distributed management has multiple points of leadership. It is a multi-agent system within which any leader can interact directly with any other leader. This form replaces the old form of management that was defined by categories of people. The favored categories were men or women, old or young, traditional or progressive, all depending on the particular group with the most power. The responsive form of leadership does not depend so much on power. It depends on relationships. With the rapid changes in data and culture, the new form of leadership depends upon wisdom and responsiveness.

Wisdom is the ability to see something from multiple perspectives and then make decisions that make sense to multiple perspectives. Wisdom isn't limited to traditional forms of power that rest solely in expertise or the potential use of force. Wisdom increases the need to govern by trust, principles or common values. Wisdom acknowledges what it is not competent to judge and avoids the temptation to proclaim policy.

Leadership training is a way to give to a few, simple tools to those who are gifted and willing to lead. For nine years I taught group leadership at Reformed Theological Seminary. My teaching may have saved some students from making some mistakes. But the most excellent leadership is seldom a result of training.

One origin of leadership comes as a special and lifelong gifting from the Holy Spirit. It is mentioned in the gifts of the Spirit

(Romans 12:8). Another type of leadership comes by willing individuals taking responsibility in a particular circumstance. Still another comes just in one-on-one relationships. Leadership does not require large groups of people. God makes all kinds of opportunities for people to lead.

There was an opportunity for Moses to lead as a senior citizen, and also an opportunity for Timothy, whom Paul counseled not to be ashamed of his youth as a leader. There was an opportunity for Samson to lead, and also an opportunity for Deborah, in a patriarchal society. There was an opportunity for Peter to lead large groups, and an opportunity for Philip to lead in a one-on-one relationship.

The church cannot afford to make up its own definition for leadership. We must stop insisting on a narrow interpretation of "servant leadership" as the expectation for every natural leader's actions, because some of the best servants are becoming de facto leaders by simply focusing on meeting needs. And while that's fine, we can't afford to overlook those with the spiritual gift of leadership. There are gifted visionary leaders who are not leading simply because visionary leaders do not fit into the practical structure the church has designed. When God's spiritually gifted leaders are not the ones leading the church it should come as no surprise that the church isn't leading the culture.

The need for leadership is too great not to be distributed. Bottlenecks for ministry training are numerous and they tend to strangle the breadth of potential church leadership. Church-generated leadership must be general and pervasive as well as specific and professional as ordained by the church. That complementarity is a necessary for successful co-leadership.

A great example of co-leadership happened in Northland, without any help or involvement of our stated organizational leaders.

In March of 2005, Daniel Bernard of *Somebody Cares Tampa*

Bay, contacted Steve Bruton from our church staff about the possibility of working a co-venture with Operation Blessing, a CBN ministry in Virginia Beach, Virginia, to bring their Dental Mission to Central Florida. In essence, Operation Blessing would provide the equipment, supplies, and expertise to provide a three-day, completely free dental services clinic. All they needed was a host organization, location, thirty to forty dentists, a similar number of hygienists and assistants, a few nurses, EMTs and lots of volunteers.

So how was Northland able to successfully organize something as complex as a dental outreach in only a matter of weeks? Once God gives us a vision to take care of a need, first, we pray. If we get the green light, which we did in this case, then we determine the location and the people needed to accomplish the mission. Once I announced from the pulpit the immediate need for dental professionals, not only did the incredible husband and wife team of Dr. Andrew and Susan Greenberg step up to say, "We can do this!" Sandy Larew, then President of the Florida Dental Hygienists Association along with more than 150 other professionals and general volunteers also signed up. Dr. Greenberg was a natural as the organizer of the professional team and his multi-talented wife oversaw the registration, eligibility specialists and general volunteers.

One thing we have learned about free service-type outreaches is that you have to be careful about how you put the word out. With the dental outreach, everyone agreed that we should promote the clinic only by flyers, posters and word of mouth. As it turned out, this was a very wise decision. We were nearly overwhelmed by the turnout. We registered over 200 people that first day, and after the second day of treatment had seen 223 people and provided over $60,000 in absolutely free dental care while referring another 30 patients with special circumstances to area dentists who agreed to see them.

The leaders involved in that outreach have continued to hold these events regularly in other parts of our city, and we are building many relationships with the leaders of those particular communities.

That event could not have happened, those people could not have been served, had I needed to be the leader that made it happen … or even one who was consulted on the project.

Connect Outside the Congregation

During the 1990s, there was a significant emphasis in management on "team leadership." That was an excellent advance from the "pastor as CEO" emphasis popular in the 1980s. And that in turn was an improvement from the "pastor as hired handyman and arranger of all congregational events" of previous decades.

The congregation members of the future will live their Christian lives connected to many who are outside the local congregation. In the new reality of a world connected, the leadership of the church will do well to be connected to leaders outside the local congregation. Such a connection will not add much more organizational responsibility—only the kind or responsibility that comes with maintaining a relationship. What it will add is influence.

The unity of ministries through the friendship of their leaders adds strength and authority to each partner. The old adage that there is strength in numbers is still true. Clusters, connected groups, have an energy about them that makes non-participants more likely to pay attention.

With the accumulation of relationships we must be wary about the age-old temptation toward political rather than relational influence. The voices that would use the gathered ministries to "take the city for God" are the same ones that would have called down a legion of angels to abrogate Christ's servant approach to salvation. The best way to long-term impact is love.

The Qualities of a Great Leader

In an era of explosive change, a successful operational (management) model will thrive by coordinating or connecting with others. The industrial-age paradigm of leadership management being about the business of organizing the inside of the institution is obsolete.

So what will be the distinguishing characteristics of future leaders? (See chart on following pages.)

The average leader increases isolation in the name of focus. The good leader builds better relationships inside the organization. The great leader inspires better relationships outside the organization (2 Corinthians 5:14-21).

The average leader builds by competition. The good leader builds by cooperation. The great leader builds by connection (Ephesians 2:13-22).

The average leader maintains helpful programs for people. The good leader multiplies helpful programs by finding the right people to lead. The great leader equips helpful people to not need programs (Luke 10:25-37).

The average church leader coaxes people into a building to hear of Christ. The good church leader sends Christians from the building to tell of Christ. The great church leader arranges sustenance for Christians to live for Christ every day (1 Corinthians 16:14-18).

The church of the future will be a "being with" church. Our regular connection to our congregation in their everyday lives, and to other Christian ministries will do much to develop our potential, their potential and the witness to the world ...

LEADERSHIP CHARACTERISTICS:

Natural Follower	Average Leader	
1. Wants to please self	1. Wants to please "superiors"	
2. Seldom thinks of "offspring"	2. Wants offspring to appreciate	
3. Wants sympathy	3. Wants support	
4. Wants to be served	4. Wants to build a team	
5. Has a need	5. Has an objective	
6. Tries to avoid effort	6. Tries to avoid surprises	
7. Speaks to own a perspective	7. Speaks from own perspective	
8. Serves self to get enough	8. Serves self so others won't have to	
9. Uses group for own purpose	9. Increases group for some purpose	
10. Works	10. Delegates some duties	
11. Activity of others is optional	11. Activity of others is central	
12. Makes decisions for self	12. Makes decisions for others	

Good Leader	Great Leader
1. Wants to exceed superiors	1. Wants to extend superiors (John 8:28)
2. Wants offspring to multiply	2. Wants offspring to further (John 14:12)
3. Wants resources to give	3. Wants to support givers (Matthew 28:20)
4. Wants to build teams	4. Wants to connect teams (John 10:16)
5. Has a theme	5. Is grasped by a vision (Matthew 26:39)
6. Copes effectively with surprises	6. Builds on surprises (John 9:3)
7. Speaks from general perspective	7. Speaks from other's perspective (John 4:29)
8. Serves others/no burden himself	8. Serves so others can too (John 13:14)
9. Guides group to benefit all	9. Connects groups for good (John 10:16)
10. Delegates with some outside integration	10. Integrates to distribute (Luke 10:1)
11. Goal is central	11. Relationship is central (John 17:23)
12. Decides with counsel	12. Chosen others make the decisions (Luke 10:17)

CONCEPTS IN CONTEXT
You, Christian, are a minister of the church.

Here are three challenges to help you personalize ideas found in Chapter Nine.

1) Get moving: It has been said that the journey of a thousand miles begins with one step. Similarly, the journey toward becoming an effective leader begins by taking one intentional step after another, "going out" into the worlds of others who need you. Ask God to show you what intentional steps you need to take and begin to step out in faith in your home, church, workplace, community and beyond.

2) God designed people to add their unique giftings to the whole church: Think about the qualities that others say they see in you. What has God given you to equip you for ministry? Through study, prayer and practice, begin to purposefully develop those giftings that He has placed in you for others.

3) Write down this prayer and consider making it a regular part of your devotional time: "Lord, let me help Your people, not in proportion to how much I know, or even how much I pray, but in proportion to how much they need."

dis•trib´•ut•ed church (di-strib-yoo-tid chûrch)

noun

- A church that centers on God and revolves around others rather than insisting that "our church" is the center of the universe. This is a "Copernican Revolution" of the church.
- Intentional distribution of the church with a goal of ultimate connection through the kind of relationship that reflects God's image.
- A network of churches sharing resources with one another, linking differences and bridging distances for the benefit of all.
- A way for the church at large to benefit from our differences, being perfected by those enough like us to be intimate yet different enough to be necessary.
- A comprehensive model in which spiritual maturity will continue to develop through generations of relationships.
- **Congregation members who spend their Christian lives connected to many who are outside the local congregation.**

verb

- Putting the resources of the church as close to people as possible, offering meeting points and access to resources, in order to assist Christians in helping others.
- Connecting to outsiders and serving them where they are, rather than getting them to join us.
- Arranging the church around the relationships of the congregation and partner ministries, rather than in and around a physical church building.
- Connecting with neighboring Christians for support and encouragement and to better serve their communities.

TEN
A Church Connected

In many leadership books, the question is asked, "Who is the customer?" It is an excellent question. While we don't normally think of the church having "customers", it would be wise for the church to consider the point of that question. In the local church, as it is practiced in the traditional sense, the customers would be the church attendees. In the church with a strong mission emphasis, the customers would ultimately be people whom the congregation members will serve. The customers for the church distributed are ultimately the people who will be helped by the beneficiaries of the congregation members' assistance. Like concentric circles Jesus talked about in Acts 1:8, we have to build the type of church that doesn't even know most of its beneficiaries because it is more catalytic than programmatic. What kind of an organization will do that?

Connection is the key to arranging the church around the relationships of the congregation and partner ministries, not insisting on everything revolving in and around the church building. The church then becomes naturally distributed (others-centered) in its interests, programs and finances. This reversal of emphasis is nothing less than the Copernican revolution of the church. It is a reorientation; it is becoming the church that centers on God and revolves around others rather than insisting on believing "our church" is the center of the universe. There are some practical actions in facilitating the transition to a distributed church.

Speak as much about ministry outside the church as inside. The teaching pastor is the architect of perception. Preach and teach on ministry outside the church walls. The second part of the Great Commandment, to "love your neighbor as yourself," was not just for individuals; it was for churches as well. After all, isn't a church an assembly of Christians getting equipped to live out the Great Commandment? Use the programs inside the walls to equip people to show the love of Christ by serving outside the walls.

Build your church outward on natural, not organizational, relationships. The church was originally expanded through the relationships of families, friends, fellow workers and neighbors. What makes us think that God has reduced His strategy to marketing and target groups? The most likely reason for people to attend a church is by invitation from an acquaintance; the most likely way to extend the ministry of the church is through already existing and valuable relationships. Such relationships best reflect the God we serve, last longest, have the most interchange and truly extend ministry.

In Chapter Five we looked at three types of complementary relationships: same mission, same methods; same mission, different methods; and different mission, different methods. Ways to serve together in those complementary relationships follow.

Same Mission, Same Methods:

- Some relationships will be integrated, forever partnerships. Such partnerships are the type of relationships that the distributed church loves to foster. The tone of this level of relationship is reflected in this traditional African greeting:

"How are you?"

"I am well if you are well."

These relationships will be among people and ministries who have the same theology, values, general goals and mission. Their unique and complementary gifts will offer mutual betterment. This is more of a covenant relationship than a working one. It is a matter of the heart, with a commitment of the will.

Same Mission, Different Methods

- **Some relationships will be intentional long-term associations.** People and ministries who have the same heart and different methods for ministry are good candidates for long-term association. They will trade ideas and resources, and have periodic fellowship through representatives. The Willow Creek Association is a good example of this type of mutual ministry relationship. Also, some local ministers associations, as well as some types of denominations, are examples of long-term association. Their desire to be identified with one another is a sample of unity in the church.

Different Missions, Different Methods

- **Some relationships are a matter of periodic "ad hoc" cooperation.** When people or organizations are so different that they could easily be enemies, yet they have mutual goals for their neighbors and the communities in which they live, they can still periodically cooperate to benefit the Gospel and the community. Christians can be salt and light by working with non-Christian groups to benefit all citizens in specific ways. For example, if Muslims and Jews and Christians all want pornographic literature covered or removed from the shelving at the checkout counter, then all benefit by being willing to work together to reach this common goal. The results of such efforts may produce mutual respect among congregations.

- **Some relationships are simple friendships.** Agreement on theology, method or long-term mission is not necessary in simple friendships. However, these relationships do link people and ministries that are consistently working toward the same goals. Churches that link with local charities or businesses or governments to serve the community are simple friendships with a purpose.

Remember that, for a Christian, serving with other Christians is a form of worship (Romans 12:1-2). Worship is too important to be restricted to a pew on Sunday morning. When mutual service happens in broadening circles of friendships, cluster groups with mutual interests naturally arise. These informal groups don't need a name, elected officers or a permanent bank account. When possible, make Christian relationships opportunities for worshiping together. Breakthroughs in communication technology are enabling entire congregations to worship together over great distances. Worship doesn't need to depend on how many people can assemble in "the proper" place. It hasn't depended on that since the time of Jesus (John 4:21, 23-24). Worship is the point of life. We will be worshiping in eternity, so it is the most important activity of this life too.

Keys to Connection

There are three main ways of linking to people and ministries: **theological, personal** and **organizational.**

Theological

Accurate theology enables us to build genuine intimacy with God and with other believers. If people have that relationship with God, they are our eternal brothers and sisters whether we know them personally or not.

Therefore, we will partner most closely with those who have a personal relationship with God through Christ's gift of salvation, understanding who God is in accordance with the doctrines summarized in the Apostle's Creed. Yet, constant focus on refinement of theological doctrines does not bring intimacy, or spread the love of God to people in need. For a Christian, theologically screened relationships require us to ask ourselves this question, "Do the people I'm with in this relationship help me love God with all my heart and soul and mind?"

Personal

Since we are made for relationships (as God is a relationship— Genesis 1:26-27), the most natural linking comes with those whom God gives a heart connection, as well as a complementary role. Of course marriage has a unique place among all relationships, and commitment of husband and wife is the best reflection of the oneness available to us in a relationship. Close friends can also help and renew us for the Lord's work. These relationships are personal and fulfilling.

We will partner most closely with those who renew our hearts and souls. Relationships that bring personal joy and love enable us to give the most to other people who need us. For a Christian, personal relationships require us to ask ourselves this question, "Do I enjoy the person I'm with in this relationship?"

Organizational

Since we are still on earth to accomplish our part in "loving our neighbor as ourselves" (ministry and service), and to spread the Gospel into all nations (evangelism), our most practical linking comes in cooperating with others to accomplish projects and achieve mutual goals. Service-oriented relationships are not limited to theological agreement or personal intimacy. More accurately termed "co-operations", service relationships are aimed at beneficial results for a community or the solution of a particular kind of problem. "Power consists in one's capacity to link his will with the purpose of others, to lead by reason and a gift of cooperation," was the way Woodrow Wilson addressed the value of cooperation in a letter to Mary A. Hulbert in 1913. A cooperative relationship is based on a mutual effort, short- or long-term, to accomplish something that is good for all people and will "bless … all the families of the earth" (Genesis 12:3). This type of cooperation may be with other Christians, those who carry the banner of another religion, or with non-believers. Organizational relationships require us to ask ourselves this question, "Will the people I'm in this relationship with help me help others?"

Guidelines for Potential Partners

People interested in partnering with Northland ask, "How do you build a partnership with others?" The more leaders and congregants that are directly involved, and the more vision, time and resources are shared, the more closely we can partner with a church, group or individual. Here are our guidelines for the process of partnering:

Guideline 1: The closer they are to Christ, the more closely we can partner. This calls for discernment, but it is important to spend most of our partnership energies with those who are passionate about Christ.

Guideline 2: The more people are involved from both groups, the more closely we can partner. The more numerous the points of connection the better.

Guideline 3: The more we know about each other, the more closely we can partner. Knowledge increases with consistency of contact. For individuals or groups from distant and difficult cultures, a liaison that will mediate understanding between the groups may be required.

Guideline 4: The more we can serve others together, the more closely we can partner. Serving others together teaches us much about our complementary roles, bringing us closer while expanding the Kingdom.

From Geography to Biography

The local church with a mission program may be reaching out to others, but it understands relationships in terms of "us" and "them" (no matter how dear "they" are to "us"). At the same time, it gives the illusion of being fully involved with the outside world, thereby camouflaging the need to actually be outside with others.

The local church is where most of us start, and our local congregation will continue to be our church family. But how do we begin to make the transition to "outside" relationships actually becoming an indispensable part of how we define our "inside family"?

The process to becoming "distributed" is fourfold:

1. **We need to go from "here" to "there" in our reference point.** Ministries have either internal or external targets. The leadership must consistently speak about places and cultures that are outside the congregation. American Christians must stop seeing ourselves as the center of God's world. We are blessed to be a blessing. As we think about other places and cultures we will grow less likely to gauge the effectiveness of our personal religious journey only by how much our own lives are improved. In a distributed church, the welfare of others is a reference point for personal well being. Christ laid down His life and challenged His followers to do the same.

2. **Repeatedly replace "here to there" thinking with "here and there."** In other words, make others not only a reference point, but also an aspect of our identity. The difference between a local church with a mission emphasis and a church distributed is both simple and immense. A local church can spend time and money investing in other ministries, but only when ministries beyond the walls of that church and the church itself mutually include each other in their individual identities is there a complete relationship.

If you were to write a letter to Northland Church you would send it to a singular address in Longwood, Florida. But when the congregation gathers for worship on a weekend, it gathers there and at many of other sites. Northland Church meets at multiple sites, including thousands of homes via Webstream Worship ("Northland at"). Via technology, we are one congregation worshiping concurrently and organized under a singular elder board. Additionally, though, many independent congregations have another type of relationship with us ("Northland with"). Local churches from various denominations in the United States and abroad link with us to share specific aspects of ministry. Some link with us for worship, some for mission trips, some for local work projects, etc. So when news comes from places our partners live, places like Egypt, Namibia, South Africa, Sri Lanka or Ukraine, that is our church news as well. Our prayer lists, news updates and special offerings are increasingly intermingled.

3. **There must be a transition from orientation to attentiveness.** The connection will become a way of closeness, then deference. We go from "here" to "hear." We go from "there" to "their." That is not just a clever play on words; that is the mind of Christ. At first this process feels like an artificial one, not unlike the process for making new friends. Initially, we are either trying to think of what we have in common or we are working to accomplish a goal together. Ultimately, though, in the words of Jesus, the greatest love is having a friend for whom we will "lay down our life."

4. **Long-term impact from consistent interaction becomes much more significant than we could have imagined.** Going wide, that process of going beyond ourselves to someone else is the essence of both the Great Commandment and the Great Commission. If we arrange our lives and our churches to have an outside reference point, we will be conformed to the image of Christ and we will see His power made perfect through our limitations.

Such progress takes patience; each relationship has its own timetable. Scientist James Doran said, "Comprehensive models are built, if at all, by many hands over many decades." The distributed church is a comprehensive model in which spiritual maturity will continue to develop through generations of relationships.

It is in its infancy, and may be toddling for decades to come. It will be developed in many ways, by many partnership clusters, led by many different leaders along the way. The church distributed is elastic enough that no one can predict how many forms it will take. All we know for sure is that we were made to serve Christ together.

Developing a capability that is effective both globally and locally cannot be rushed. It takes a long time, and many contacts, to build relationships over distance, and to equip others to do so. In physics we learn that there are forces that act over great distances. Gravity is one, and I would submit to you that love is another. Speed breaks down the force of gravity, and so it is with love. "But let patience have her perfect work, that ye may be perfect and entire, wanting nothing" (James 1:4 KJV).

Relationship Adjustments

Relationship adjustments may be required on occasion. Each of the four churches in which I have been a pastor occasionally required such internal and external relationship adjustments, but their occurrence never ceases to surprise me. Then I am surprised that I am surprised!

Relationships that become oppositional may not be easy, but they can still be beneficial. First, we can learn and improve from the bits of truth nestled in most criticisms. Second, we mature as leaders when we can continue to love others after feeling the sting of their hostility. When our agape-type love (unconquerable good will) is tested we have the opportunity to more wholly be like Christ. And third, if we continue to concentrate on the good that we can do, refusing to be distracted by trying to justify ourselves to those who oppose us, God will bless the good and beneficially use the negative.

How Different People Can Work Together

People who see how differences fit together will benefit not only their own cause, but also mankind in general. Those who know the necessity of variety as a basis of achievement will experience the greatest advancement. And that is especially true in a globalized world because there are more and more boundaries being bridged.

All systems are inclined toward equilibrium (no net change over time). Yet this status quo condition is the very one that makes systems vulnerable. The tendency for individuals, churches, businesses, nations and cultures to be satisfied with the familiar and the comfortable is observed in most scientific studies. Yet, so is the danger. Ludwig Von Bertalanffy states:

> "Biologically, life is not maintenance or restoration of equilibrium but is essentially maintenance of disequilibria. ... Reaching equilibrium means death and consequent decay."[21]

The local church, with its predictable programming, can be a haven of stability and reliability. Yet, if it is to have increasing life, and relevance to a changing world, it must have more than consistency. The very steadiness that is its strength for the present is its weakness for the future. Differences found in relationship with others, whether inherent ones or pop-ups along the way, add vibrancy.

There are some very good resources as well as agencies that help individuals and groups form successful partnerships. When we intentionally combine differences instead of just blend similarities, keeping those relationships positive ones is easier if we keep a few basics in mind.

- **There must be a common purpose beyond the relationship itself.** God brought Eve to Adam to embrace a purpose broader than intimacy; i.e., tending the garden. The job was not more important than their intimacy—it was integral to it.

Attention must be given to the overarching purpose of the relationship.

- **There must be clarity of roles eventually.** Just as the Trinity has different roles for different Persons in the Godhead, so too each person in a relationship must be aware of what his or her role contribution will be. While it is not necessary to detail such a matter at the beginning of the relationship, it is helpful to have some general ideas of what each party offers. Clarity comes as people work together, and adjustments are made according to recurring contributions and needs.

- **There must be a common source of authority, not government.** A relationship cannot depend upon government (an instrument of force) for its unity, but it does need a refuge of appeal for conflict resolution. Authority that has the beneficence of God will usually be a mutually respected person, or an agreed upon document of order, or a common heritage that serves as a reference point. What it cannot be is a rule enforcement process that makes the parties obey, rather than help them be responsible to settle their own disputes with humility and the guidance of the Spirit. Only the latter builds relationships.

- **There must be a recurring expression of respect and appreciation for the other.** The key to intimacy is people well-appreciated. Scripture implies that women will perceive this appreciation as love, and men will perceive it as respect (Ephesians 5:33). In either case, a bonding ingredient for differences is consistent expressions of high regard for the other. Just as worship binds us and orients us to God, so too, in a subordinate sense, appreciation binds two or more parties together.

- **There must be a continued communication beyond the utilitarian.** Nothing builds togetherness like communication that is built on something other than a want or a need. If the only time we go to God in prayer is when we are in need of something, our relationship with Him will be very frustrating and shallow. If the main goal of our conversations with our partners is utilitarian, the relationship shrivels. That is true even if the conversations are about what kind of support they need. It is important to have conversations that indicate our personal interest in their lives.

- **There must be a sense that God called you together into a covenant relationship.** This last ingredient is central, and the most encouraging for the long run. It will be the most important reason for people with great differences to stay together. Only those Jews who realized the fulfillment of their original calling from God (Genesis 12:3) involved the Gentiles and could abide with the Gentiles. Lasting unity in ministry depends upon a sense that God called you together forever.

Having stated these basics, let me make perfectly clear that this is not a "to-do" list. Personal relationships are not built by to-do lists. There is something almost romantic about the unity that results from the welcoming of differences. Relationships that have differences at their core will not survive if mechanical maintenance of details becomes a focus.

The pressures generated in any relationship, but especially those working with great differences, are relieved in large part by seeing the value of the distinct differences in a larger perspective. Differences appear to be huge and irritating when only viewed as differences per se. They are seen as complementary and purposeful when viewed as a part of God's larger plan ...

CONCEPTS IN CONTEXT
You, Christian, are a minister of the church.

Here are three challenges to help you personalize ideas found in Chapter Ten.

1) Our connections to one another will not be built by to-do lists, but by practical expressions: You can begin by speaking as much about ministry outside the church as inside. Consider some ways that you can do this.

2) Think about the other churches and ministries in your community: Ask God to help you to begin forging relationships with others. If there is a venue where local ministers from various backgrounds get together to discuss mutual challenges and opportunities, then join in. If such an organization doesn't exist, then consider starting one yourself!

3) Consider the guidelines for potential partners included in this chapter: Using this information as a grid, begin to consider which people outside your normal circle of influence might become a potential partner. Set up a time to meet and to discuss how you might join together in common causes.

dis•trib´•ut•ed church (di-strib-yoo-tid chûrch)

noun

- A church that centers on God and revolves around others rather than insisting that "our church" is the center of the universe. This is a "Copernican Revolution" of the church.
- Intentional distribution of the church with a goal of ultimate connection through the kind of relationship that reflects God's image.
- A network of churches sharing resources with one another, linking differences and bridging distances for the benefit of all.
- A way for the church at large to benefit from our differences, being perfected by those enough like us to be intimate yet different enough to be necessary.
- A comprehensive model in which spiritual maturity will continue to develop through generations of relationships.
- Congregation members who spend their Christian lives connected to many who are outside the local congregation.

verb

- Putting the resources of the church as close to people as possible, offering meeting points and access to resources, in order to assist Christians in helping others.
- Connecting to outsiders and serving them where they are, rather than getting them to join us.
- Arranging the church around the relationships of the congregation and partner ministries, rather than in and around a physical church building.
- Connecting with neighboring Christians for support and encouragement and to better serve their communities.
- **Reorienting ministry efforts from inside to outside, from solitary to partnered, to an arrangement that constantly reminds us of God.**

ELEVEN
A Church Someday Soon

Because we were made for relationships, individuals and churches will go beyond themselves, when life would be simpler alone.

Someday Soon

Someday soon, because we are the children of the infinitely patient and precise God, who for centuries has been crafting us to be more like Him, the structure of the church will reflect the image of God, not the image of medieval, feudal hierarchies or industrial age corporations. We will see that trinity is a model for organization; a reflection of the God we worship. We will know that the prideful separation caused by sin diminishes not just our personal lives but also our group's method of operation. Churches will be integrated in their activities, not inhibited by their hierarchy.

Because we were made for relationships, local churches will have a distributed identity both as one body and as several bodies. The church will draw near to people's everyday lives. You and I will be actually working together, because in this age, "having been built on the foundation of the apostles and prophets, Christ Jesus Himself being the corner stone" you and I, "being fitted together … are being built together into a dwelling of God in the Spirit" (Ephesians 2:20-22).

This will happen no matter what our geographical distance, no matter what our denominational distinctive, no matter what our political predisposition, no matter what the size of our church, no matter what our role in ministry, no matter how skilled or broken our ability, and no matter what our social status.

We are being fitted together so that we might be related in the most effectual way. Understanding that we have been prearranged for cooperation, for the purposes of Christ, will be a motivation for our togetherness. Understanding that we are intentionally distributed, not accidentally scattered, will be a pronouncement that what has appeared to be division and chaos is meant for multiplication and coordination.

Someday we will realize the mission is a reminder of our need to belong to each other. As extensions of each other, we are never unproductive, for what I am not doing, you are doing. What one does not get accomplished, another will. There is only "one body and one Spirit … one Lord, one faith, one baptism, one God and Father of all who is over all and through all and in all" (Ephesians 4:4-6).

Together we will finally realize that God has made no mistakes in our placement, in our gifts, in our circumstances or in our past. They are all strategic for such a time as this.

That means that just as God sent out Abram to build a people for Him and to bless all the world (Genesis 12:1-3), He will send out His church and our earthly travels will help bond His family together. And it will be again just as it was when Jesus sent out the disciples into all the world to build His church distributed in different places (Matthew 16:18, 28:18-20, Acts 1:8, 1 Corinthians 1:2). Just as the early Christians visited each other to bond the congregations of the church together (2 Corinthians 8:18-24) we will be visiting with each other, not in order to build our own church but to build the other's ministry and to build the church universal by supporting each other in the process.

The day is coming when groups will seek to cluster together for mutual advantage over the hardships of life. In all of God's Creation, the church is among the last to learn this principle. From cells to insects, from animals to teenagers, from political groups to businesses, the benefits of close relationships have been used to survive and thrive in a hostile environment. It has been used to build the most advantageous basis from which to nurture offspring. Ministries are beginning to understand this advantage.

We will seek to serve all, but especially those given to us in a close relationship. We will see the relationship as more important than the activity. We will see other ministries as close family, and we will, by our clustering together, be of benefit to the world, not just to each other.

Even when it comes to other religions, rather than participate in destructive competition, Christians will be grace-filled witnesses of the God who cares for them. We will realize that we do not convert them, the Holy Spirit does; we will do our part by living like Christ among them.

The day is coming when the global culture will be more open to the Gospel than ever before. Not only has modernity left the world spiritually empty, but also the uncertainty of post-modernity has the world actively searching for anything that will last.

We live in a world asking for spiritual realities. It is a world rapidly connecting with personal communication devices but still wondering what we have in common. We live in a world where science is seen less as the savior, and religion is viewed as "helpful for some," but where many people are still longing for unchanging truth.

We live in a world of so much information that the most valued people are not the bearers of information anymore but those who can interpret it in a way that makes sense for everyone.

God aligns the capabilities for such unity. For increasing numbers of us today, He is diminishing our hostility toward differences and increasing our sympathies toward each other. He is rebuking us by the examples of some nations, churches and religious groups that compete against each other. He is letting us ponder the horrifying example, especially in the Middle East, of what happens when ethnic and religious groups refuse to find a way out of territorial wars.

We strengthen our identities as Christians when we cooperate with non-Christians for the good of everyone. We will associate with Christians who are not like us as well as partner with Christians who have the same vision as ours. We will build partnerships with Christians who want to build permanent relationships for the work of the Gospel.

Someday soon we will participate in a global movement connecting the church, and local church identity will not be lost—it will be enhanced. It will not be for the sake of the church only, but for our witness to the world. As flexible and enjoyable as a Tinkertoy™ bridge, the church will show the world, in an inviting way, how to span differences. There will be close and long-lasting relationships of cooperation for the purpose of serving.

Someday soon we will realize that close relationships affect everything. They not only determine how we witness to the world but also determine how much we know. Relationships will be seen as instrumental in understanding complete truth.

Even now, many Christians link together for long-term support and effectiveness. And there are pastors and parachurch ministry leaders who meet together regularly because they see their ministries' efforts and their personal efforts of service enhanced through the connection. Sharing people and resources, experiencing common worship services that link up different states, even different continents—it's all already happening. And there is no governing body making it happen. It is happening because of the Holy Spirit's superintendence and many Christians have begun to see from a perspective bigger than their own. I am praying that someday soon, all Christians will be brave enough to leave familiar territory to venture toward their God-given mission.

EPILOGUE
A Church of Adventure

When I was a young boy, our family always went to the same place for our vacation. It was a lake in the northern peninsula of Michigan that had a row of little cabins on its shore. The area was largely undeveloped. Descendants of Indians still lived there. Our favorite nighttime activity was to go to the dump and watch the bears eat garbage.

Back then it was not unusual for extended families—aunts, uncles, and grandparents—to vacation together. The men loved this spot because it had good fishing and it was cheap. The women did not like it because, in the words of my grandmother, "We have to do everything here we have to do at home, only without the appliances."

One particular summer, I was hoping for something really special. My long-widowed Mom had recently married. Herb was very conservative and careful in his approach to everything, but he was also a caring and accommodating person. I could tell that I caused him to be a little nervous because I was not at all cautious in the way I lived life, and I was not the least bit coordinated. So I knew that my vacation dream would be a real test for my new dad.

I wanted to drive the boat. Cabin renters could rent the old wooden boats at the docks. These were leaky, smelly, dead-worms-floating-in-the-bottom boats, just the kind a fisherman loved. The renter supplied his own motor, and it was his choice if he wanted his boy to drive the boat—at least that is what I told my dad as we traveled all the way from Ohio.

Before leaving the dock, Dad carefully arranged our family in the boat. My mom was at the bow, my sister and I were on the middle plank, and my dad was at the stern operating the motor.

Finally, after all my begging, my dad said, "Okay, Joey. I want you to stand up very slowly—not yet! And step very cautiously toward me, then sit beside me on the other side of the motor's handle. Do you understand? Okay, slowly now … slowly, that's it … good. Now, take your hand and place it on top of my hand that is on the motor's handle. Good. Now I will slowly remove my hand, and you take the motor's handle, but do not move it. Is that clear? Good. Here we go."

I held the handle in place.

After approximately thirty seconds of having my hand on the motor's handle, his hand slipped in again to replace mine, as he instructed me to slowly return to my original seat. He was sure he had given me the thrill of a lifetime. I was deeply disappointed but, of course, did not express that to my good-hearted dad.

As we returned to the dock, my grandfather read the expression on my face. He had been sitting on a bench, looking at the beauty of the lake. He knew immediately what had happened. He said to me, as I walked up the dock, "Joey, come up here and sit by me." I was glad to do that.

Pop said, "You know, I was just thinking about something. You see that island way out there?"

"Yeah, Pop, I see it."

"I was just thinking, maybe no one has ever explored that island. Maybe no human foot, except for maybe an Indian's, has ever walked there. Maybe there are snakes and bears and poison plants on that island. It sure would be good to have someone really brave go and explore that island for me. I can't go because I've got a weak ticker, ya know, but if I could find someone younger, someone adventurous enough, I'd send him over there to tell me what is on that island."

"Pop!" I shouted, with what I thought was a brilliant and original idea, "I am younger and brave! I could go and explore that island for you!"

He looked like the thought had never occurred to him. "Well, Joey" he thought for a moment, "You know, that is a great idea! Would you do that for your old Pop?"

"Sure!" I said, trying not to jump out of my skin. "But, Pop, I don't think Dad would let me drive the boat over there."

"Well, you could take my bo— "

He did not get the entire word out of his mouth before I was in his boat speeding toward the frightening, unknown, wild territory. I was so scared and so exhilarated. I thought of turning back. After all, there could be hungry beasts or hostile Indians there. If I turned back, though, what would my grandfather think? He was counting on me.

I went ahead. I trembled with each step, but I lived.

Day after day, I would bring him discoveries from the island: Squirrel remains (from which Pop, an old veterinarian, would teach me animal anatomy); red berries ("Don't put those in your mouth, Joey, I bet that two of them could kill an elephant!"); and feathers ("Do you suppose this was part of an Indian war bonnet?")

The chance to feel like a discoverer, a pioneer of sorts, was thrilling. Even better, however, were the conversations and the feelings of closeness I shared with my grandfather. I became, from that summer on, an explorer at heart.

I will never forget the chance for adventure and learning Pop gave me that summer. I have often wondered if there would ever be an opportunity to explore new worlds again and learn as I go.

Now we are all speeding toward an unknown future. It's no secret that the church must learn to walk in an unfamiliar environment. I, for one, am thrilled about it. However, as I face this other unknown territory, the future, I am remembering the one thing I wish I had during those trips—some other kids to go with me. It would have been less intimidating and more fun. So, who wants to go?

Frequently Asked Questions

What are some key shortcomings of the present form of doing church that demand a new form of church?

We know from Scripture that the church will still exist when Christ returns and we can see that, remarkably, the present arrangement of doing church has lasted for seventeen centuries. The early church, in the first three centuries, took the form of distributed groups that were linked together. When the church became an institution, starting in the fourth century, it slowly developed patterns that would be effective only in a top-down society. Whether the political structure of society was in the form of an empire, a feudal kingdom or a nation, the church was arranged to be one of the institutions within a hierarchical worldview.

The top-down church will not be effective in the world of the future for at least four reasons:

1. Though leadership will always be crucial to the development of people, the function of a leader is switching from director to catalyst. He or she must be more empowering than instructive, more generally encouraging than "orders issuing." Of course, even with these new assignments the leader retains the servant role described in Luke 22:25-27.

2. Though information will always be valuable in the pursuit

of truth, the traditional method that emphasized a teacher giving students information is switching to one in which the excellent teacher is the one who can help interpret the information nearly everyone can access.

3. The growth of the church is no longer mainly happening in the Western world where hierarchy has been a main component in the culture. With the rapid growth of the church in South America, Africa and Asia, cultures that place great value on community and group relationships, we will see forms of church structure around the globe being contextualized into more relational arrangements.

4. Inspirational leadership, through preaching and the example of some Christians' lives, will continue to be catalytic. The capability of leaders, though, to actually direct many others in their decision making will decrease in proportion to the speed of the changing world and the explosion of knowledge. Few people have the capability to know exactly what others should do, because it is a different world daily. Thus, the best thing leaders can do for people in their spheres of influence is to teach them the biblical truths: tell them who God is and what He has done. Teach biblical values, general principles for decision making, and help them with ways to stay constantly in touch with the leading of the Spirit.

How is the church distributed different from a denomination?

Church distributed exists to further the Kingdom on earth by building relationships that can benefit everyone for God's glory. Relationships matter greatly and partnerships between ministries that have compatible theology, philosophy and mission are vibrant in a distributed church model. Unlike a denomination, the church distributed is not organized under a legal hierarchy. Partnerships can

Partnerships can take place inside, outside or across denominational boundaries. Each cluster of partnerships is independent, yet all are part of a movement to connect the church for greater efficiency and unity. In short, the church distributed is not a "nondenominational denomination."

What are the main components of a distributed church not found in other churches or denominations?

The distributed church depends on relationships, not organizational agreements. While "covenant agreements" are possible and even admirable to maintain local church membership or denominational connections, the distributed church is only as strong as the relationships it enables. Human relationships have an emotional "expiration date" and must be renewed to remain vital. The relationships that characterize the distributed church are those formed for the sake of ministry to others, not those formed mainly for mutual edification or organizational growth.

The distributed church is formed for the sake of continually connecting those outside and different from itself. The local church believes its greatest effort should be invested in the congregation, and a denomination believes its main efforts should be invested in those affiliated within an ecclesiastical family. The distributed church exists for the sake of those not yet included or not yet connected with each other. We believe that God has already providentially distributed His people among all the peoples of the world. Our job is to call them to be His church, connect them together and, as well, to connect existing ministries, to reflect His oneness (John 17:21, 23).

Traditional churches are led by appointed leaders who direct their groups. The distributed church sees its members as ministers who need more encouragement to walk out the calling God has given them than they need pointed direction. It is field-based in its organizational development. The leaders serve the believers who are distributed to be salt and light in the world. The distributed church is also a learning organization that re-forms often to better support the Christians who are serving others.

This sounds like it is complicated. Is it?

It is no more complicated than becoming great friends. One of the attractive things about church distributed is that any church can do it right now. Denomination, size, location—none of that matters in deciding whether or not a church will "go distributed." What does matter is the desire to reach out to others and support them in their ministry. Just as individuals within a congregation appreciate efforts by the organized church to encourage and support them in their everyday lives, so do entire ministry organizations appreciate encouragement and support, and it doesn't need to be financial.

Can we be a church distributed if our local congregation doesn't have great togetherness itself?"

In one sense, a church cannot be a healthy partner without first being a healthy local church. And yet a local church, like an individual, cannot be healthy without connection to others. The very nature of a distributed church prompts the need for connections from inside and outside itself. The paradox that Northland found is that this model of church prompts unity. Northland Church has never emphasized closeness in community as much as we have since we decided to be in partnership with other ministries. In essence, our emphasis outside the walls is a catalyst part of connecting inside the walls.

How will the distributed church clusters be governed?

The distributed churches or ministries do not need any authority over them other than what has already been established by their will usually be an organizing, or lead church, in a cluster, but the leadership is informal rather than formal.

How does the distributed church benefit 'non-churched' Christians more than the local church model can?

The numbers of people who consider themselves Christians but are not affiliated with any local church is staggering. In this paradigm, Christians who do want to connect with other Christians without walking into a church building can do so. The connection with other Christians, not the building, is the expression of the church. The distributed church gives Christian groups a way to link with an organized church. Christians in a "habitual" meeting (Hebrews 10:24-25) wherever that is, can connect to the organized church for worship services and resources.

How will the distributed church be financed?

There is no one treasury to which everyone needs to contribute. Every covenant partnership, or every project, will include the details of who is to pay for what. Each party will contribute with the goal of the others' support in mind (2 Corinthians 8:1-5). Any church can work with practically any outside group on almost any project for any length of time. As relationships grow, resources are shared, people are blessed, and a distributed church is taking form.

How will the distributed church develop?"

Since the distributed church links people and resources, it develops by extending already established relationships and welcoming new ones. Our strength is in partnering with any group of Christians that can take the Gospel into the world. Isolation is a real problem, not only for most individual Christians but also for most churches, and the distributed church model comes out of a desire to link those who feel alone in their journey of faith.

How is this different from a large church helping smaller churches?

Churches such as Saddleback and Willow Creek continue to be tremendous examples of large churches teaching, encouraging and resourcing smaller churches. They have focused on principles that can make any church more effective.

The distributed church emphasizes mutual service-based ministry. Both inside and outside such a congregation, the grace of God comes through the relationships built on mutual service. God brings together particular people that He uses because of their complementary differences, not specifically because of what they know or how competent they are. These relationships are mutually beneficial, not one-directional in teaching and receiving.

Aren't you afraid of heresy when you are partnering on the basis of complementary differences instead of doctrine or denomination?

Partnerships are among those who have a personal relationship with God through Christ's gift of salvation, understanding who God is in accordance with the doctrines summarized in the Apostle's Creed. Having said that, as I mentioned in Chapter Ten, focus on refinement of theological doctrines is not what brings intimacy or conveys the love of God to people in need. It is our experience that most Bible-based groups have within them people who can spot heresy (over-emphasis of some partial truth) very easily. In the distributed church, as in any Christian church, the preaching and teaching must be biblically sound. When it is, and Bible study is the priority for equipping the congregation, the groups will have within their constituency theological watchdogs who will question how far the boundaries of each cluster should be expanded. The participants have responsibility for orthodox theology, and church leaders must be willing and able to address issues that are brought to them for clarification. Partnerships, by their very nature, are not lived out in a vacuum.

Is there a biblical model for forming clusters of churches and ministries in the distributed church?

The Scripture seems to record the linking of churches on a practical basis (Acts 15, 2 Corinthians 8-9, et al), but the interchange presumes an ontological (one that expresses our/His nature) connection. In other words, family members link with other family members when there is a special need because they are the family of God.

Of course one of the most historic and biblical references is the natural and geographic connection of the city-church (example: "the church at Corinth"—1 Corinthians 1:2). The Bible has repeated references to the church in a city. That is indeed a legitimate basis for forming a close and mutually beneficial relationship among ministries. The problems with such a relationship come with the size of the cluster. Practically speaking, in a larger city there are too many churches to have close and consistent interchanges.

The other categorization of the church mentioned in the Scripture is called the "house church," or "*oikonomos.*" For example, "Priscilla and Aquila ... the church that is in their house" (Romans 16:3, 5). Today, those churches may indeed find a practical necessity for bonding with other churches. Yet, because of their independent nature, it may not be a natural tendency for them to band together with each other or to be an active part of the city church.

The barriers to ongoing relationships with other churches in each of these affinity groupings are not mainly theological, or even practical, but personal. The distributed church celebrates the legitimacy of both the city church and the house church. The clusters built among the distributed churches may be a way of overcoming the "too many to be close" problems of the city church, and the "too small to get connected" problems of the house or very small church.

The partners in a cluster have the same responsibilities as those in any healthy and practical group. There must be:

- A leader/organizer/initiator ministry that forms a cluster small enough that all the participants can regularly and personally support each other.
- Liaisons between the ministries that make the connection human rather than structural.
- Long-term partners who have more interest in supporting each other in ministry than they have in just doing projects together.

Who can initiate a distributed church cluster?
You and your church can.

Footnotes

1   Shaffer, Richard A., "Sun Was Right: Why the Network Is What Matters," *Fortune*, June 12, 2000. p. 32.

2   McDermott, Gerald R., *One Holy and Happy Society*, Pennsylvania State University Press, University Park , PA 1992, page 97.

3   Capra, Fritjof, *The Web of Life*, Anchor Books, New York, NY 1996, pages 29-30.

4   Medina, John, *The Outer Limits of Life*, Oliver Nelson Publishing, Nashville, TN 1991. p. 47.

5   Sowell, Thomas, "Culture and Equality," Hoover Digest 1998.

6   Blocher, Henri, *In the Beginning*, InterVarsity Press, Downers Grove, IL 1984. p. 102

7   Waldbauer, Gilbert, *Millions of Monarchs, Bunches of Beetles*, Harvard University Press, Cambridge, MA 2000. p. 235.

8   Eisenberg, Evan, *The Ecology of Eden*, Vintage Books, New York, NY 1998. p. 9, 10-11.

9   Cohen, Don and Prusak, Lawrence, *In Good Company: How Social Capital Makes Organizations Work*, Harvard University Press, Cambridge, MA 2001. p. 4.

10 Ibid. p. 16.

11 Latourette, Kenneth Scott, *A History of the Expansion of Christianity: The First Five Centuries*, Vol. 1, Harper Brothers, New York, 1937. p. 51,52,54.

12 Ibid. p. 79.

13 Ibid. p. 100.

14 Ibid. p. 116.

15 Stark, Rodney, *The Rise of Christianity*, Harper Brothers, San Francisco, CA 1997. p. 74, 86.

16 Latourette, *A History of the Expansion of Christianity: The First Five Centuries*, Vol.1 p. 356.

17 Ibid. p. 356

18 Walker, Williston, *A History of the Christian Church*, Charles Scribner's Sons, New York, NY, p. 319.

19 Latourette, *A History of the Expansion of Christianity: The First Five Centuries*, Vol.1 p. 430.

20 Ibid. p. 430.

21 Bertalanffy, Ludwig Von, *General System Theory*, George Braziller Publisher, New York, NY, 1968. p. 191.

All Scripture is from the New American Standard Version unless otherwise indicated.

Bibliography

Achtemier, Elizabeth and Paul. *Interpreter's Dictionary of the Bible*, Nashville, Tennessee: Abingdon Press, 1962.

Aczel, Amir. *Entanglement: The Greatest Mystery in Physics*, New York: Four Walls Eight Windows, 2001.

Axelrod, Robert. *The Evolution of Cooperation*, New York: Basic Books, 1984.

Bacon, Francis. *Advancement in Learning*, Glacier, Montana: Kessinger Publishing, 1994.

Barabasi, Albert-Laszlo. *Linked: The New Science of Networks*, Cambridge, Massachusetts: Perseus Publishing, 2002.

Blocher, Henri. *In the Beginning: The Opening Chapters of Genesis*, Leicester, England: Inter-Varsity Press, 1984.

Brafman, Ori and Beckstrom, Rod. *The Starfish and the Spider: The Unstoppable Power of Leaderless Organizations*, New York: Penguin Group, 2006.

Brierley, Peter. *Future Church: A Global Analysis of the Christian Community to the Year 2010*, London: Monarch Books, 1998.

Buchanan, Mark. Nexus: *Small Worlds and the Groundbreaking Science of Networks*, New York: W.W. Norton & Company, 2002.

Chen, Ming-Jer. *Inside Chinese Business: A Guide for Managers Worldwide*, Boston: Harvard Business School Press, 2001.

Cunningham, David. *These Three Are One: The Practice of Trinitarian Theology*, Oxford, UK: Blackwell Publishers, 1998.

Doz, Yves, and Hamel, Gary. *Alliance Advantage: The Art of Creating Value through Partnering*, Boston: Harvard Business School Press, 1998.

Drucker, Peter. *Managing in the Next Society*, New York: Truman Talley Books, 2002.

Drucker, Peter. *Post-Capitalist Society*, New York: HarperBusiness, 1993.

Etzioni, Amitai. *From Empire to Community*, New York: Palgrave Macmillan, 2004.

Ferber, Jacques. *Multi-Agent Systems: An Introduction to Distributed Artificial Intelligence*, London: Addison-Wesley, 1999.

Friedman, Thomas. *The Lexus and The Olive Tree: Understanding Globalization*, New York: Farrar, Straus and Giroux, 1999.

Friedman, Thomas. *The World Is Flat: The Brief History of the Twenty-First Century*, New York: Farrar, Straus and Giroux, 2005.

Gunton, Colin. *The One, The Three, and The Many: God, Creation, and the Culture of Modernity*, Cambridge: Cambridge University Press, 1993.

Helgesen, Sally. *The Web of Inclusion: A New Architecture for Building Great Organizations*, New York: Currency/Doubleday, 1995.

Heslam, Peter. *Creating A Christian Worldview: Abraham Kuyper's Lectures on Calvinism*, Grand Rapids: William B. Eerdmans Publishing Company, 1998.

Hiebert, Paul. *Anthropological Reflections on Missiological Issues*, Grand Rapids: Baker Books, 1994.

Jencks, Charles. *The Architecture of the Jumping Universe: How Complexity Science is Changing Architecture and Culture*, London: Academy Editions, 1997

Nye, Joseph, Jr. *The Paradox of American Power: Why The World's Only Superpower Can't Go It Alone*, Oxford: Oxford University Press, 2002.

Nye, Joseph, Jr. *Soft Power: The Means to Success in World Politics*, New York: Public Affairs, 2004.

Olasky, Marvin. *The Tragedy of American Compassion*, Wheaton: Crossway Books, 1992.

Pavlicek, Russell. *Embracing Insanity: Open Source Software Development*, Indianapolis: Sams Publishing, 2000.

Roberts, Bob, Jr. Glocalization: *How Followers of Jesus Engage a Flat World*, Grand Rapids: Zondervan, 2007.

Schwartz, Peter. *The Art of the Long View*, Doubleday Books, New York, New York, 1996.

Sweet, Leonard. *Post-Modern Pilgrims: First Century Passion for the 21st Century World*, Nashville: Broadman & Holman Publishers, 2000.

Walls, Andrew. *The Cross-Cultural Process in Christian History*, Edinburgh: Orbis Books, 2002.

ABOUT NORTHLAND,
A CHURCH DISTRIBUTED

Northland, A Church Distributed is an innovative congregation of more than 12,000 that utilizes technology to connect Christians through concurrent worship. People worship weekly at interactive sites throughout Central Florida. Additionally, each weekend, some 1,500 sites throughout the world connect to the church via live Webstream Worship.

The church's sanctuary, completed in August 2007, has the capability to provide "virtually unlimited seating" through technology and offers in-house seating for 3,200.

Following the distributed pattern set by the early church, people in Northland's congregation take leadership of nearly every ministry effort inside the church, out in the community and abroad. Elders, pastors and paid staff don't try to control the ministry initiatives of congregants or the connections they make, and, they don't watch over their shoulders unnecessarily. Dr. Joel C. Hunter encourages those who worship with Northland: "Do what you can, where you are, with what you've got." And they do!

To learn more about this unique congregation or to participate in live worship, visit www.northlandchurch.net.

ABOUT THE AUTHOR

Since June 1985, Dr. Joel C. Hunter has served as senior pastor of Northland, A Church Distributed.

Before bringing his family to Northland, Dr. Hunter served as a United Methodist pastor for 15 years in Indiana. He and his wife, Becky, are parents to three sons and have been partners in the ministry since their marriage in 1972. Becky is the president of the Global Pastors' Wives Network and is the author of *Being Good to Your Husband On Purpose*.

A longtime bridge builder who seeks common ground for the common good across denominational, ethnic and political lines, Dr. Hunter approaches today's issues in a biblical and balanced manner. In addition to serving on the board of the World Evangelical Alliance, he serves on the executive boards of the National Association of Evangelicals and the Global Pastors Network.

Dr. Hunter has become a nationally known spokesperson for "Compassion Issues" outlined in Scripture: sanctity of life, creation care, justice, poverty, and marriage and the family. Learn more at www.northlandchurch.net/joelhunter.

All proceeds from this book will go to Northland's new facilities, built to celebrate our God and connect us with others.